Eyewitness
TREASURE

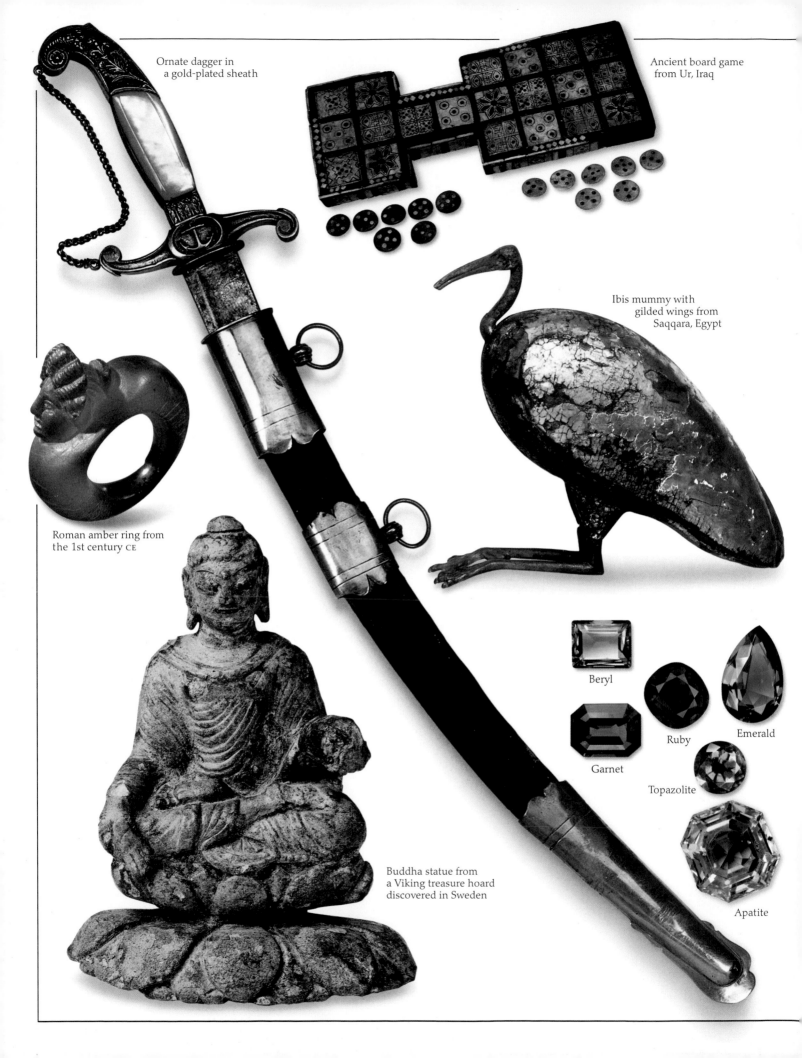

Ornate dagger in
a gold-plated sheath

Ancient board game
from Ur, Iraq

Ibis mummy with
gilded wings from
Saqqara, Egypt

Roman amber ring from
the 1st century CE

Buddha statue from
a Viking treasure hoard
discovered in Sweden

Beryl

Ruby

Emerald

Garnet

Topazolite

Apatite

World's first coins, minted
2,600 years ago in Lydia (now Turkey)

Oldest known representation
of a human face, found in
Brassempouy, France

Eyewitness
TREASURE

Written by
PHILIP STEELE

Steel replica of an
Anglo-Saxon helmet from
Sutton Hoo, England

DK Publishing

Limestone bust of
Queen Nefertiti
of Egypt

Diamond Sutra from
Dunhuang, China

DK

LONDON, NEW YORK, MELBOURNE, MUNICH, AND DELHI

Consultants Dr. Carenza Lewis, Britt Baillie

Senior editor Rob Houston
Editorial assistant Jessamy Wood
Managing editors Julie Ferris, Jane Yorke
Managing art editor Owen Peyton Jones
Art director Martin Wilson
Associate publisher Andrew Macintyre
Picture researcher Louise Thomas
Production editor Hitesh Patel
Production controller Charlotte Oliver
Jacket designers Martin Wilson,
Johanna Woolhead
Jacket editor Adam Powley
US editor Margaret Parrish

DK DELHI

Editor Alicia Ingty
Designers Mitun Banerjee, Arijit Ganguly
DTP designers Tarun Sharma, Preetam Singh
Project editor Suchismita Banerjee
Design manager Romi Chakraborty
Production manager Pankaj Sharma
Head of publishing Aparna Sharma

First published in the United States in 2010 by
DK Publishing
375 Hudson Street, New York, New York 10014

10 11 12 13 14 10 9 8 7 6 5 4 3 2 1
175395—01/10

Copyright © 2010 Dorling Kindersley Limited

A catalog record for this book is available from the Library of Congress.

ISBN 978-0-7566-6037-6 (Hardcover)
ISBN 978-0-7566-6038-3 (Library Binding)

Color reproduction by MDP, UK, and Colourscan, Singapore
Printed and bound by Toppan Printing Co. (Shenzhen) Ltd., China

Discover more at
www.dk.com

Bronze bell
from China

Pike from the
Thirty Years' War

Black figure-ware vase from ancient Greece

Roman
Catholic crucifix
from Italy

Spanish gold doubloon

Contents

Jeweled egg with a miniature
elephant by Peter Carl Fabergé

Precious treasure

Since prehistoric times, people have loved to decorate themselves and their homes with beautiful and precious objects. These treasures may be made of gold or silver, diamonds, emeralds, ivory, pearls, beads, or feathers. People have always collected treasure and hidden it away, to keep it safe. Sometimes explorers and archeologists discover rich treasure hoards in lost cities, ancient tombs, or shipwrecks. These offer us a glimpse of past glories. Who made these objects and why? Were they made for people who wanted wealth, power, prestige, or beauty? Were they made to glorify the gods? Were they fought over or stolen by warriors or looters? Treasure forms part of our history—and part of our dreams.

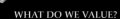

WHAT DO WE VALUE?
Precious metals or coins are not the only measure of wealth—treasure can be made up of whatever people consider to be valuable. The Māori of New Zealand made necklaces from sharks' teeth. They also used them for trading and exchange. People in other lands have used shells, salt, or even cocoa beans as forms of money.

Scrolled vine leaf pendant, possibly from France

TREASURE FROM THE TOMB
In 1922, an archeologist named Howard Carter discovered a tomb in Egypt's Valley of the Kings. It belonged to Tutankhamun, a young man who ruled Egypt from around 1347 BCE. In the dark passages and chambers of the tomb, Carter discovered jewelry, gold, ebony and ivory, thrones, fans, trumpets, and weapons. The treasure was placed there for the dead pharaoh to take on his journey to the next world.

Eyeball skewers may represent a fierce gaze

MASK OF DEATH
This spectacular mask was made about 1,000 years ago by the Sicán people who lived in northern Peru. It was placed on a mummified body. The gold and the dangling ornaments tell us that it belonged to a very important man of the Sicán culture. In many parts of the world, gold indicated royalty or nobility, and it was often associated with the gods. Very little is known about the Sicán culture, since most of their treasures were looted by grave robbers in the 1900s.

Nose ornament, a symbol of high status

Ear spools (ornaments worn on the ear lobes) were a badge of nobility

Red cinnabar paint was probably used to protect the dead person in the afterlife

VIKING HOARD

Viking warriors sailed far from their homes in Scandinavia, trading, fighting, and raiding. They attacked rich towns and looted monasteries. Some stayed on in the lands they raided, while others returned to their homes with the wealth they had collected. Sometimes archeologists still discover hoards of Viking treasure, buried for safety in times of trouble. This Hon treasure was found in a bog in southeast Norway in 1834. It dates from the 860s and includes 5½ lb (2.5 kg) of gold objects, as well as some silver and glass beads. There is a finger ring from England, a neck ring from Russia, and a finely crafted gold brooch from France, as well as Roman, Byzantine, Anglo-Saxon, Frankish, and Arabian coins.

Arm ring from Russia

Gold brooch from France

Neck ring from Russia

Arabian coin

GOLDEN SHRINE

Some of the finest treasures in Europe may be seen in churches and cathedrals. This dazzling shrine can be viewed in the Cologne Cathedral in Germany. It was made between 1181 and 1225 and was designed to hold what Christians believed were the bones of the Three Kings who had brought gifts to the baby Jesus. These holy relics were previously held in Constantinople (Istanbul, Turkey) and Milan, Italy.

RAISED FROM THE SEABED

Deep beneath our oceans are the remains of ships, from Roman galleys to Spanish galleons. These wrecks have attracted archeologists and treasure seekers alike. Divers may discover ancient cargoes, silver coins or gold bars, jeweled caskets, cannon, or anchors. The search for sunken treasure is expensive, but it brings rich rewards. The treasure can also be a key to help us unlock the mysteries of the past. When and where did people trade? How did they build ships or work metal?

Earliest treasures

In the Stone Age, before people learned to work precious metals, they created treasure. As they gathered food or followed the herds of wild animals they hunted, they collected stones, shells, seeds, and feathers. From these they made jewelry. Shell beads found at the Blombos Cave in South Africa are believed to be 75,000 years old. Some carved stones were probably used for magic—perhaps the shape of a female body would bring fertility to those who wanted children, or the shape of a bison might capture the spirit of the animals hunted by the tribe.

MAMMOTH IVORY
This tusk from a mammoth was carved into the shape of a bison during the Stone Age. It was found at a site in the Russian town of Zaraysk. The site was occupied at various times between 23,000 and 15,000 years ago. Other discoveries there included a necklace of fox teeth and flint knives.

THE FIRST LADY
This is the first known carving to show the human face in a realistic style. It was carved from mammoth ivory about 25,000 years ago and is just 1½ in (3.8 cm) high. Was this an important lady such as a priestess, or perhaps a goddess? The carving was found in a cave in Brassempouy, France. Such finds are priceless treasures, because they show us the ancient origin of human values and beliefs as well as artistic skill.

THE HUNTED BISON
The year is around 12,000 BCE. A bison turns its head, and the moment is captured forever in a carving. This treasure of Stone Age art was found at La Madeleine, Tursac, southwest France. It is made from reindeer bone and is 4½ in (11.4 cm) high. The animal almost seems to be alive, caught in a stampede or a chase. Bison were widely hunted for food in Europe at that time.

EVERLASTING JADE

This is a *cong*—a hollow cylinder-shaped artifact, most likely used in rituals. It was made in eastern China between 3300 and 2250 BCE and was carved from jade, which was valued above all other materials in China. Jade was such a hard, long-lasting stone that it was associated with eternal life. Jade objects were specially carved to be placed in graves.

Jade was polished with quartz and engraved with a finely pointed flint

THE THINKERS

These figures were found at a burial site at Cernavoda, Romania. They were modeled from clay at the end of the last Ice Age, in around 10,000 BCE, but have a rather modern look to them. We do not know for sure why they were made. They seem to show a man and woman lost in thought, but they may represent rulers or have some religious meaning.

Fine details were etched into bone with a sharp stone knife

AMBER FROM THE BALTIC

This Stone Age carving of a head was found near Asarp, Sweden. Ancient treasures were often small so that they could be easily carried or stored. Materials were valued for their feel and their appearance. On beaches people may have found pieces of shiny black jet, or amber in glowing shades of yellow or orange. Amber, which is actually fossilized tree resin, was common around the Baltic Sea in northern Europe. It could be made into beads for jewelry or sewn onto clothes.

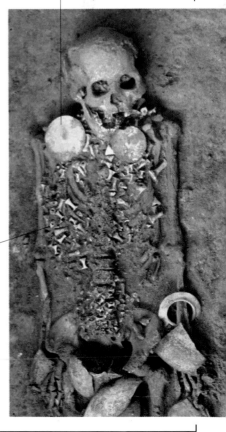

Shoulder disc made of shell

More than 120,000 shell beads had been sewn onto a cape

THE SHELL PRINCESS

This woman lived more than 3,500 years ago beside the Bang Pakong River, which flows into the Gulf of Thailand. Her community ate rice and shellfish and used the shells to make tools and beautiful jewelry. Her grave was discovered with more than 150 others at a site called Khok Phanom Di. She must have been a very important person, because she was buried with all her finery, including beads, bracelets, and other decorative items, all made from shell.

A glint of gold

METALS THAT SHINE catch the eye, and gold gleams more than any other. Gold can be worked and reworked very easily. It is soft and can be beaten or hammered into shape without being heated. It was one of the first metals to be worked by humans and was highly prized in most parts of the ancient world. Over the ages humans learned the art of hot metalworking, or smelting. They began to work with other metals, such as silver and copper, and learned how to mix metals into alloys such as bronze. Precious metals, such as silver and gold, were used to make statues of the gods, royal crowns, and coins for the marketplace. Nonprecious, or base, metals, such as iron, were often tough and ideal for making tools or weapons, but they could also be used to fashion beautiful, long-lasting treasures.

Gold ore

THE CRUCIBLE
Molten gold is poured into a mold from a red-hot container called a crucible. When the metal cools, it will become a solid bar, or ingot. Metals are mostly found embedded in rock, known as ore. The ore must first be discovered, then mined, and finally, heated to extract the metal in a process called smelting. Metals were being worked in western Asia as early as 6000 BCE. To ancient peoples, these new technologies seemed magical, perhaps even the work of gods.

Holes allowed the pieces to be stitched to clothes

THE VARNA TREASURE
A 6,000-year-old burial ground at Varna, Bulgaria, has been excavated since 1972. So far, about 3,000 pieces of gold, including animal shapes, beads, disks, earrings, bracelets, masks, and a ceremonial ax, have been found. These bulls were made before the invention of smelting, and the gold was beaten flat and then embossed (hammered to make raised decorations).

Varna bulls were symbols of power and strength

Winged lion protects the owner from evil

Early coins were stamped with a symbol of the city or its ruler

Punch marks certify that the coin has been weighed

THE LION'S SHARE
This splendid gold horn, or rhyton, might have been used for drinking or for pouring offerings to a god. It was crafted by a master goldsmith between 500 and 400 BCE. It is one of the treasures discovered in Iran at Hamadan, which was part of the mighty Persian Empire. This city was visited by the royal court each year.

MEASURES OF WEALTH
The first known coins were made more than 2,600 years ago in Lydia (now in Turkey). Early coins were made from precious metals such as gold, silver, or electrum (a natural alloy of the two). They could be easily carried in a small pouch and so were perfect for buying and selling goods. They could also be stored and hidden as treasure.

Stamp and punch marks transform the metal into a coin

*Pattern of lotus
flowers and buds*

*Battle scene with
armored warriors*

*Fine-toothed
comb*

GOLDEN WARRIORS

Tattooed Scythian warriors galloped across the steppe grasslands of eastern Europe and central Asia 2,400 years ago. They buried their dead rulers in mounds known as *kurgans*, which were piled high with treasure such as cups, weapons, and gold collars. This 5-in- (13-cm-) high comb was found in the Solocha mound, in the valley of the Dnieper River in Ukraine.

*Tapered horn
with ribbed
sides*

*Wings transform
the lion into
a ferocious
celestial creature*

MAGICAL METALS

In ancient Asia and medieval Europe, scholars known as alchemists believed it was possible to turn base metals into gold. They tried all kinds of magical spells and experiments, but in vain. Although many alchemists were frauds, some made genuine scientific breakthroughs, such as the discovery of carbon dioxide.

BULLION WORTH BILLIONS

Welcome to Fort Knox, Kentucky. This building holds about 4,600 tons (4,180 metric tons) of gold bullion, or bulk metal, mainly in the form of ingots. Today, most of our money transactions are carried out using paper, plastic, or a computer keyboard. However, most countries still keep a reserve of solid bars of gleaming gold. It is a safe investment in times of economic crisis.

*Design mimics
the shape of
drinking vessels
made of
antelope horns*

Jewels and jade

METALS MAY GLEAM, but diamonds are cut and polished so that they sparkle, scattering light. Gemstones offer color—deep reds, pinks, pale yellows, greens, and blues. Pearls have a delicate creamy sheen. Jade comes in various shades of green. Throughout history, these beautiful dazzlers have been set in crowns, diadems, earrings, rings, necklaces, bracelets, brooches, pins, daggers, and swords. They have been sewn onto clothes and gloves. They have encrusted holy shrines and been inlaid in marble monuments. Jewels have become symbols of love and marriage, of beauty and allure, of power and wealth. They have been associated with particular human characteristics, good fortune, or deadly curses.

St. Edward's sapphire

Decorations include 273 pearls

RARE AND COSTLY
The value of gemstones and pearls depends on their size, appearance, and rarity. Most gemstones are minerals created deep inside Earth under high pressure and intense heat. They are mined and then cut, polished, or treated to look beautiful. Pearls are created by oysters inside their shells. They are not gemstones but are just as valuable.

Emerald

Beryl

Scheelite

Apatite

Ruby

Phosphophyllite

Topazolite

Amethyst

Black Prince's ruby spinel

Garnet

Peridot

Cerussite

Pearls

Heliodor

Cullinan II diamond, part of a massive diamond discovered in 1905

Ruby spinel

CROWNING GLORY
This British crown contains 2,868 diamonds. It is topped by the St. Edward's sapphire first worn by King Edward the Confessor in 1042. The giant ruby belonged to Abu Said, ruler of Granada in present-day Spain. He was murdered by Pedro the Cruel of Castile, also in present-day Spain, who passed the ruby on to Edward, the Black Prince of England, in 1367.

Amber is soft and easily carved

Wind-up elephant can walk and move its trunk

Diamonds in a pinecone pattern

Key

JEWELED EGG
This magnificent egg is made of gold, silver, diamonds, and brilliant blue enamel. Enamel is made by melting powdered glass onto a surface, giving it a shiny coating. Inside the egg is a toy elephant. The egg was made in 1900 by Peter Carl Fabergé (1846–1920), one of the most famous jewelers in history. Fabergé eggs were commissioned by emperors Alexander III and Nicholas II of Russia, who gave them as Easter gifts to the empresses Maria and Alexandra.

RING OF HEALTH
This Roman ring, made of amber, is about 1,900 years old. Many Romans believed that wearing amber could prevent or cure all sorts of illnesses. Rich deposits of amber, which is fossilized tree resin, were found on the Baltic coast and passed along trading routes to northern Italy. Much of it came to Aquilea, a town that specialized in making jewelry from amber, ivory, and gemstones. Amber was also carved into lucky charms and little boxes.

2,156 jade tiles sewn with gold thread

Burial suit of Dou Wan, the Jade Princess

ALL COVERED IN JADE
Jade, the most precious stone in China, had been placed in tombs for thousands of years, in the belief that it would preserve the body forever. Eventually, whole burial suits of jade were crafted for the royal family. These were made of small tiles secured with gold or silver thread. Made in 113 BCE, the burial suit of Prince Liu Sheng contained 2,690 green jade tiles. A similar suit was made for his wife, Dou Wan.

Diamond studs

Blue is the bowerbird's favorite color

Crown has 11 emeralds

BLING-BLING
This cell phone is made of gold and studded with diamonds. Bling, a slang word, was invented by hip-hop music stars to mean flashy jewelry or other glitzy accessories. In the 21st century, some sports celebrities, movie stars, and other moneymakers love to show off their new wealth, just as much as Scythian warriors and medieval princes did long ago.

BIRDS LIKE BLING, TOO!
The satin bowerbird lives in Australia. When a male wants to attract a mate, he builds her a bower out of sticks. He decorates this with any colorful or shiny material he can find, including flowers, stones, foil, plastic, coins, or glass. Magpies and jackdaws are also famous for placing shiny objects in their nests, even stolen rings or other jewelry.

The finest things

ALL KINDS OF PRECIOUS handmade items are considered treasure. We may admire these for the skill with which they were crafted, for their beautiful appearance, or for the value of their materials. People in the past desired to own such items every bit as much as gold and silver. Royal treasures found at ancient sites such as Ur in Iraq or the Valley of the Kings in Egypt include gaming boards, musical instruments, fans, belts, sandals, bows, and arrows. Such treasures may also be valuable simply because they are rare and difficult to acquire. In museums we can see samples of rich tapestries, costumes and textiles, intricately carved wood, engraved metals, fine pottery, enamel, and glass. Over the ages only a handful of such treasures have survived breakage, rot, rust, dust, or damage by insects.

WEST AFRICAN BEAUTY
About 600 years ago, this carved ivory mask would have hung from the hip of Esigie, the *oba* (king) of Benin, in what is now Nigeria. It was worn for special ceremonies and represented his mother, Idia. The color of ivory was a symbol of purity, linked with the sea god Olokun.

Golden thread adorns a silk bag from the 1920s

FABULOUS FEATHERS
Was this headdress worn by Moctezuma II, who ruled Mexico in the days of the Aztecs? We cannot be sure. It was certainly part of the treasure that was looted and sent back to Europe by Hernán Cortés, whose Spanish soldiers defeated the Aztec Empire in 1521. The long green feathers were plucked from the tails of living quetzal birds. The quetzal was a sacred bird in ancient Mexico, associated with the great god Quetzalcoatl.

SHIMMERING SILKS
Silk, spun from the cocoons of moths and woven into fine cloth, was first made in China thousands of years ago. It was exported to western Asia and Europe along a network of trading routes called the Silk Road. Silk represented the height of fashion and luxury. Designs could be woven into the silk. These patterned silks were mainly traded at Damascus, Syria, and so became known as damask.

Crimson silk damask, 1700s

A MĀORI TREASURE BOX
The Māori of New Zealand used beautifully carved wooden boxes, or *waka huia*, to store their most treasured personal belongings, such as greenstone pendants, combs, and feathers. Because these items were in contact with the body, other family members had a sacred duty not to touch them—it was taboo (forbidden). The treasure box was therefore hung up among the rafters of the house.

Pattern showing horsemen and elk

PRECIOUS SOUND
A violin might not be everybody's idea of treasure—unless it is a Stradivarius like this one, made in 1729. Many musicians believe that these violins, made by the Stradivari family of Cremona, Italy, have a unique tone. That might be because of the density of their wood. In 2006, a Stradivarius was sold for $3.5 million.

MAGIC CARPET
This richly patterned carpet was found in the burial mound of a Scythian prince who died in the Pazyryk valley, in Siberia's Altai Mountains. It is the world's oldest known knotted carpet, dating back to the third or fourth century BCE. Each yard of the carpet contains 360,000 knots, so it would have taken a skilled craftsperson a long time to make, adding greatly to its value. The carpet has survived only because of the region's bitterly cold climate, which preserved it under a thick sheet of ice. Some experts believe that the carpet was made by Scythians. Others think it was brought to Siberia from Persia (modern Iran). Western and central Asian carpets have long been treasured around the world for their beautiful colors, patterns, and fine craftsmanship.

Quetzal feather

Dog-shaped porcelain flask

PORCELAIN FROM THE SEA
This flask, along with some 6,000 pieces of porcelain, or fine china, was recovered in 2004 from the wreck of a Portuguese trading vessel that sank 400 years ago. The porcelain dates back to the Ming dynasty (1368–1644), a period of Chinese rule famous for its pottery. Porcelain was treasured by people in the Western world because they did not know how to make it. The fact that it was so fragile also added to its value.

Gold

Royal splendor

RICH AND BEAUTIFUL OBJECTS do not just show how wealthy someone is. From the earliest times, they have also been used to show status—the position that somebody holds in society. The most impressive objects of all were designed to show off the power of the chief, the king, or the queen. Headdresses or crowns were placed on the head. Ornate weapons or staffs were grasped in the hand. Rich costumes, cloaks or furs, jeweled belts, collars, or rings were worn as emblems of power. These symbols of rule are called regalia, from the Latin word for "royal things." Regalia form an important part of the treasure dug up by archeologists or displayed in museums.

Golden crown

Ceremonial staff, or scepter

Royal orb

Carved wooden throne

THE CORONATION
Richard II of England was crowned king at the age of 10, on July 16, 1377. His crown was a symbol of royalty. His orb represented the world, with a cross for the Christian faith. The scepter was an ancient sign of authority. Kings wore long robes trimmed with the white fur of the stoat, or ermine.

Crimson robe

Carvings depict a king's great victories over his enemies

ROYAL TUSK
This tusk of elephant ivory was carved around 1750. It was kept in the ancestral altar of the kings of Benin, in present-day Nigeria. All sorts of items have served as regalia over the ages. They include umbrellas, fly whisks, ostrich plumes, horse tails, feather headdresses, embroidered hats, swords, and shields. Flags, banners, or standards may proclaim the presence of a king or queen.

Orb with a cross

Royal crown

Five-clawed dragon

DRAGON ROBES
Chinese emperors during the Qing period (1644–1912) wore robes of silk. Each one of these took more than two years to stitch. A five-clawed dragon design was reserved for the emperor himself. Princes and some noble members of the royal court could wear a four-clawed dragon, and lesser officials a three-clawed dragon. Yellow was the color of imperial rule and could be worn only by the emperor or with his permission.

MIGHTY MACE
The mace was originally a weapon—a kind of war club. It later became an ornamental symbol of royal or civic power. A mace is still displayed in the parliamentary chambers of some nations with a monarch as the head of state, such as the United Kingdom, Canada, and Australia. These parliaments cannot meet without the mace being displayed.

Ocean waves embroidered in silk

Diadem with precious stones and pearl pendants

THE EMPRESS IN HER JEWELS
This mosaic from Italy was made around 547 CE. It pictures Empress Theodora, wife of Emperor Justinian I. They ruled the east Roman, or Byzantine, Empire, which had its capital at Constantinople (Istanbul, Turkey). The Byzantine court was famous for its diadems (jeweled headbands), crowns, and luxurious silks. These regalia were influenced by western Asian styles. Byzantine fashions in turn set the style for kings, queens, and religious leaders across Europe during the Middle Ages.

Wooden shaft covered in silver gilt

Jeweled collar

Robe dyed purple, the imperial color

Painted wooden lid

Chalice, a cup used in Christian worship

TREASURE CHEST
This wooden chest comes from the Château de Chillon, a medieval stone castle beside Lake Geneva, Switzerland. During the Middle Ages, strong chests with locks were used to store coins, clothes, and all kinds of other precious goods. Kings and queens transported chests containing coins around the country in wagons so that they could pay their servants and soldiers.

Ornamental base

Medieval key

Sacred treasure

MANY RELIGIONS CONDEMN people who love money too much, who are greedy for gold, or who hoard treasure for themselves. However, many of the finest treasures have been made by people wishing to honor their gods or ancestral spirits. All over the world people build shrines and make religious objects, such as incense burners, candlesticks, prayer beads, musical instruments, statues, and stands or cases for holy scriptures. They use precious metals and jewels to craft these items. Places of worship have become rich treasure houses. Some people feel that sacred, or holy, treasures are a distraction from true belief. They prefer to worship in simpler surroundings.

TIBETAN BUDDHA
This joyful statue, made in Tibet in the 1800s, shows Queen Mayadevi, the mother of the Buddha, resting against a tree just before she gave birth to the Buddha. It is made of gilded bronze and decorated with colored stones.

Bowl for alms

Sheet of gold, hammered and cut

Young Buddhist monks

GIVE UP YOUR WEALTH
These young Buddhists are training to be monks. They have given up all personal wealth and carry bowls for alms (contributions of food or money) from the public. The Buddha was born a prince around 563 BCE, but he taught that desire for material possessions such as gold and jewels causes unhappiness.

ALL GOD'S GOLD
The world's leading religions have splendid, often ancient buildings in which to worship. Some of these have golden roofs, carved stone and statues, beautiful mosaics, and paintings. Jewish synagogues contain the menorah (a seven-branched candle holder), a lamp, and the ark that holds the Torah, or scriptures. Islamic mosques display in calligraphy (fine writing) the sayings of God's messenger Muhammad, as well as prayer rugs and stands for holding their holy book, the Qur'an. Christian churches feature stained glass windows, altars, and crucifixes (models of the cross on which Jesus Christ died). Hindu temples often display richly painted, carved, or decorated statues of the gods.

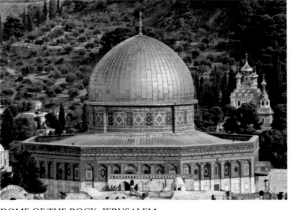

DOME OF THE ROCK, JERUSALEM
The city of Jerusalem is sacred to Jews, Christians, and Muslims. This gleaming Islamic shrine, the Qubbat As-Sakhrah, built between 685 and 691 CE, is the oldest surviving Islamic building in the world. Its dome, originally made of gold, has been restored with a shining alloy of bronze and aluminum.

GOLDEN TEMPLE, AMRITSAR
Glinting in the sunshine, the Harminder Sahib at Amritsar in north India is the holiest site in the Sikh religion. Completed in 1604, it is famous for its gold exterior. Its greatest treasure is the original Guru Granth Sahib, the holy scripture of Sikhism.

Silver frosted with gold

The figure reminded worshipers that Christ had died for them

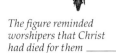

Raised pattern beaten out from behind

Engraved names of the apostles, who first spread Christ's teachings

Sun God headdress

Roman Catholic crucifix

A SACRED SUNBURST
To many of the ancient peoples in South America, gold represented the Sun God, the bringer of life and energy to the world. This spectacular headdress would have been worn on the forehead of a high priest or ruler around 1,800 years ago. It was discovered near La Tolita, in the delta of the Santiago River in Ecuador.

ARDAGH CHALICE
In 1868 two Irish boys were digging up potatoes on the site of an ancient fort at Ardagh when they uncovered this chalice. It was made for Christian monks in the 700s CE. The silver chalice is decorated with gold, brass, pewter, and enamel work.

ITALIAN CROSS
This ornate crucifix was made from silver in 15th-century Italy. Churches were filled with such treasures, many of them costly gifts from people who wanted God to forgive them for their sins.

CATHEDRAL OF THE ANNUNCIATION, MOSCOW
At the heart of Moscow's medieval citadel, the Kremlin, stands the Cathedral of the Annunciation. Built in the 1480s, its gilded domes are in the traditional style of the Russian Orthodox Church. It has precious holy images called icons, wall paintings, bronze doors, and a floor of jasper.

SHWEDAGON PAGODA, YANGON
The ancient mound, or pagoda, of Shwedagon contains sacred relics and is covered in gold given by Burmese Buddhists. At the top is a huge diamond, and beneath that 5,448 other diamonds and 2,317 rubies. The pagoda also has shrines, bells, and images of animals.

VENKATESWARA TEMPLE, TIRUPATI
This ancient temple in south India honors Lord Vishnu. A great center of pilgrimage for Hindus, its riches include all kinds of gold ornaments as well as sacred statues and images.

Pigments and pages

Pigments are the colors used in making dyes, paints, and inks. They were once made from costly and rare materials, such as saffron, cinnabar, and brazil wood. Writers, scribes, or artists applied pigments to paper, or to all kinds of other surfaces, such as clay, papyrus (made from reeds), vellum (made from calf skin), linen, canvas, wood, or plaster. More than 200 calf skins might have been needed to produce just one book in the Middle Ages. Copying a text in the days before printing often took years. Books may have had rich bindings in leather or gold, and paintings too may have been framed or paneled with silver, pearls, or precious wood. However, the real value of art or literature lies in the magic of creativity and the inspiration offered by images or words. Paintings and books are delicate objects, unlike metals or gemstones. Their survival over hundreds of years makes them very precious objects.

TREASURES OF THE CAVES
Stone Age hunters painted these powerful images of bison in a cave at Altamira, Spain, about 17,000 years ago. The pigments they used included charcoal, ocher, and iron oxide. Sealed off by a rockfall, these prehistoric art treasures were discovered in 1879 by nine-year-old María de Sautuola and her father, Marcelino.

Angel carrying a symbol of purity

The Virgin Mary—pictured for the first time in a Western manuscript

The Buddha talking with his disciple, Subhuti

The Diamond Sutra

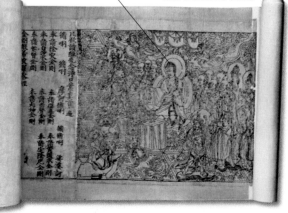

A SPECIAL SCROLL
This Buddhist scripture is known as the Diamond Sutra. It was printed, using wood blocks, on May 1, 868 CE, making it the world's earliest dated printed book. It takes the form of a scroll more than 16 ft (5 m) long. Both printing and papermaking were Chinese inventions. The scroll was stored in a cave at Dunhuang in northwest China, where it was discovered in 1907. It is precious because of its historical importance, its rarity, and its beauty.

LOCK UP YOUR BOOKS!
In this old library at Wells Cathedral in Somerset, England, the books are chained to the shelves so that they cannot be stolen. Even after printing made it cheaper to produce lots of books, many of them are still very precious objects. They are made of beautiful paper, bound using the finest leather and gum, and decorated with gold.

Étude pour "La Femme en Bleu"
(Study for "The Woman in Blue")

ART AS TREASURE
When French artist Fernand Léger painted this picture in 1912–13, he could not have imagined how 100 years later it would become a treasured object worth a fortune. When *Étude pour "La Femme en Bleu"* was auctioned in New York City in 2008 it sold for $39,241,000.

The letter "T" elaborately decorated

SWIRLING COLORS AND LETTERS
The Book of Kells is a national treasure of Ireland on display at Trinity College, Dublin. It is a book of Christian scriptures, produced around 800 CE. The book's pages are made of vellum and the text is handwritten in beautiful lettering. Illustrations, margins, and letters are decorated with intricate patterns of knots, swirls, plants, and animals. The book may have been made by monks on the island of Iona, Scotland, and then brought to the monastery at Kells, Ireland. Luckily, it escaped the Viking raiders who repeatedly attacked and looted these sites.

Gold hammered into very thin sheets of foil, or leaf

Gold leaf is brushed onto the lettering

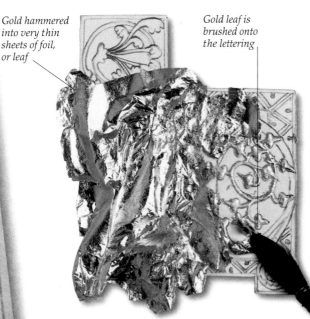

ILLUMINATION
The decoration of manuscripts in medieval Europe was called illumination (from the Latin word for "lighting up"). It was painstaking work, involving patience and skill. Inks, paints, and gums were brewed from plants, charcoal, and minerals. Blue was made from lapis lazuli, imported all the way from Afghanistan. Capital letters were made to glisten with gold or silver leaf.

Treasures in the tomb

Tens of thousands of years ago, people often placed personal possessions—or grave goods—in tombs so that the dead could use them in the afterlife. In later centuries, when chieftains, princes, kings, and queens died, mourners filled their tombs with lavish grave goods. Archeologists have discovered jewelry and regalia, weapons, armor, and chariots in graves across the world. Sometimes grave goods included animals and even people, who may have been the ruler's wives, servants, or soldiers. Most were deliberately killed, perhaps to accompany the ruler's spirit on its journey to meet the gods.

MASK OF THE PHARAOH
This mask was placed over the mummified body of Tutankhamun, the young pharaoh who was buried in Egypt's Valley of the Kings in 1324 BCE. It is made of gold, lapis lazuli, colored glass, quartz, and obsidian (a black volcanic glass). The striped headdress, with its cobra emblem and false beard, is part of the pharaoh's regalia.

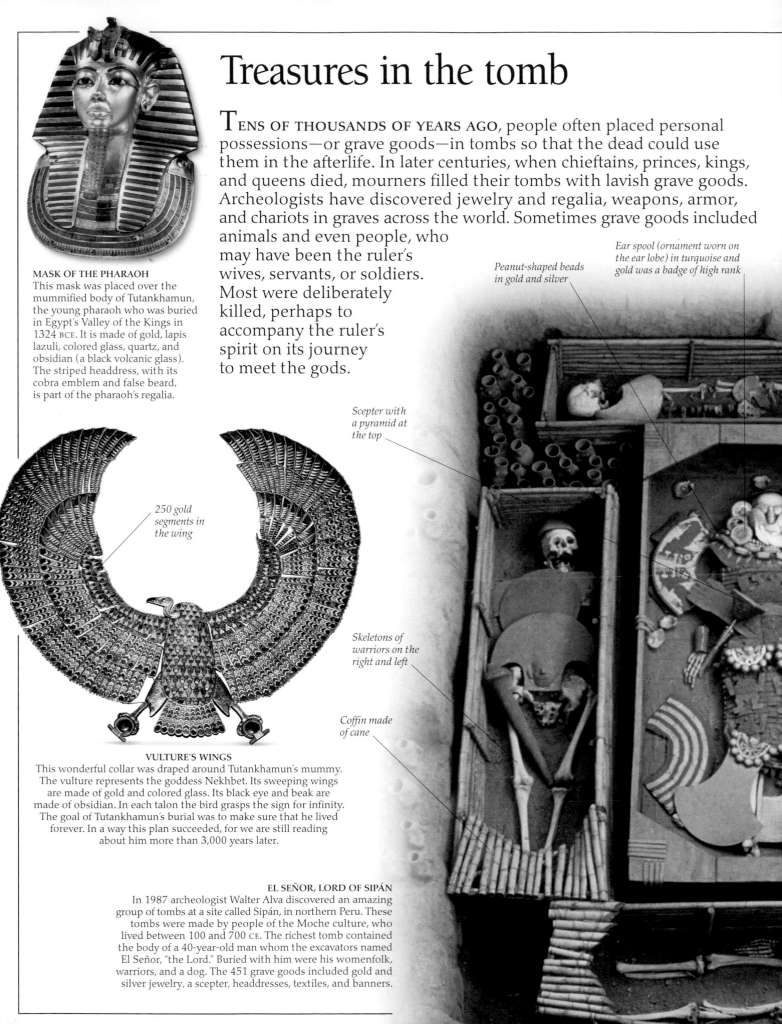

250 gold segments in the wing

Peanut-shaped beads in gold and silver

Ear spool (ornament worn on the ear lobe) in turquoise and gold was a badge of high rank

Scepter with a pyramid at the top

Skeletons of warriors on the right and left

Coffin made of cane

VULTURE'S WINGS
This wonderful collar was draped around Tutankhamun's mummy. The vulture represents the goddess Nekhbet. Its sweeping wings are made of gold and colored glass. Its black eye and beak are made of obsidian. In each talon the bird grasps the sign for infinity. The goal of Tutankhamun's burial was to make sure that he lived forever. In a way this plan succeeded, for we are still reading about him more than 3,000 years later.

EL SEÑOR, LORD OF SIPÁN
In 1987 archeologist Walter Alva discovered an amazing group of tombs at a site called Sipán, in northern Peru. These tombs were made by people of the Moche culture, who lived between 100 and 700 CE. The richest tomb contained the body of a 40-year-old man whom the excavators named El Señor, "the Lord." Buried with him were his womenfolk, warriors, and a dog. The 451 grave goods included gold and silver jewelry, a scepter, headdresses, textiles, and banners.

MUSIC FROM THE GRAVE

This musical instrument is a reconstruction of a lyre that was discovered, along with many other treasures, in the royal cemetery at Ur, an ancient city in Iraq. The lyre was decorated with a bull's head, and its soundbox, frame, and tuning pegs were plated with silver.

Bull's head covered in gold

Inlay of shell and lapis lazuli

Wooden soundbox

Skeletons of women above and below

Vessels containing food and drink

Golden headdress

Silver hip protector

RICHES OF HOCHDORF

In 1968, a Celtic chieftain's burial mound dating from 530 BCE was uncovered at Hochdorf in southern Germany. The chieftain was dressed in a birch-bark hat, Chinese silk, and gold-striped shoes. His possessions were impressive—a wagon, a cauldron that once held a honeyed drink called mead, drinking horns, weapons, and lots of gold and jewelry. The goods recovered tell us about the superb craftsmanship of the ironworkers and goldsmiths of that time.

Golden bowl and gilded iron dagger in its sheath

Brooch from Tillya Tepe representing the Greek goddess Aphrodite

GORGEOUS GODDESS

Tillya Tepe, meaning "golden mound," is a site in Afghanistan where a prince and five ladies were buried around 100 CE. About 20,000 pieces of jewelry and gold ornaments were found here. This region was a crossroads of peoples and cultures. Influences from as far as Greece, which is about 2,500 miles (4,000 km) away, can be seen in many artifacts.

Oak stern with carvings of animals

SHIP BURIAL

Seafaring peoples sometimes buried their rulers and nobles in boats. This is part of a Viking ship, nearly 72 ft (22 m) long, discovered in Oseberg, Norway. Buried in the ship were two women, fine woolen clothing, imported silks, tapestries, sleighs, a cart, bedposts, and chests. Remains of animals were also found. The mourners had covered the ship with a mound of earth to create a visible monument.

Precious offerings

IN MANY ANCIENT RELIGIONS, people made solemn offerings to their gods and goddesses. Their priests performed rituals intended to bring rain for their crops or victory in times of war. Some believed that the existence of the world itself depended on such offerings. Sometimes offerings involved sacrifice—the ritual killing of living things, even human beings. However, they could also be gifts of food, wine, incense, coins, precious jewels, or gold. Weapons could be hurled into a lake or buried to make a god less angry. Even today, people make religious offerings of flowers, light a candle when they pray, and throw coins into wishing wells to bring good luck. Archeologists call these votive offerings, and they are a fascinating form of treasure.

HEAL ME!
If you suffered from a bad leg in ancient Greece or Rome, you would offer a model of your limb at the temple of Asklepios, the god of healing, in the hope that he would cure you. Similar offerings are made today at Christian shrines in the Mediterranean region.

A TWO-WAY CONTRACT
Ancient Egyptians believed that their gods would protect them from harm, both in life and after death, especially if they wore a special amulet or charm. This falcon amulet is a symbol of the god Horus. In return for this protection, people gave the gods gifts of food, holy water, statues in the shape of people and animals, and objects of personal value.

Gilded disk represents the Sun

Golden offering from Chichén Itzá

THE SUN WAGON
People in northern Europe used to cast sacrifices and votive offerings into lakes and wetlands. This model of a horse-drawn chariot pulling the disk of the Sun was deliberately placed in a bog at Trundholm, Denmark, around 1300 BCE. In many cultures, the Sun was believed to ride a chariot across the sky.

THE WELL OF SACRIFICE
This deep pool, known as a cenote, was a site for human sacrifice about 1,000 years ago. It is in the Mayan city of Chichén Itzá, Mexico. The Maya also threw their treasures into the pool as offerings to the gods. During the 20th century, archeologists dredged up a haul of jade, obsidian, silver, copper, carved stone, beautiful gold face ornaments, masks, and many human bones.

Golden bowl from Chichén Itzá

THE CUTTING EDGE

This ceremonial knife is called a *tumi*. It was made by a craftsman of the Chimú people, who ruled northern Peru from the 900s to the 1400s. The knife was not itself an offering. It was probably used for the sacrifice of humans or animals such as llamas. The handle may represent a god named Naymlap, who was believed to have been the ancestor of the Chimú rulers.

Gold set with turquoise and chrysocolla stones

TREASURE HOUSE OF THE GODS

Delphi is an ancient Greek holy site, with many temples. People from all over Greece traveled to Delphi to hear prophecies from a priestess and make rich offerings to the gods. Each Greek city built its own storehouse in Delphi to hold these treasures. This is the treasury of Athens, built of marble about 2,500 years ago.

Mare made of bronze

Spoked chariot wheel

Rounded blade of solid gold

MONEY TO BURN

The people of Vietnam have a new year (Tet) tradition of burning fake paper money and incense sticks as an offering to ancestral spirits. They also burn paper models of luxury goods such as televisions and cell phones as offerings. In China, people place coins and banknotes on religious statues. These modern treasures are all offerings, and they follow a tradition that is thousands of years old.

Hidden hoards

FOR MUCH OF HISTORY, there were no bank vaults to keep people's wealth locked safely away. When invading armies rampaged through the land, people buried their most precious possessions for safekeeping and fled. They hoped to come back and dig them up later. But sometimes they were killed, or could not return, and their belongings remained buried for centuries. Treasure hidden in this way is called a hoard. Such hoards were also buried by robbers trying to conceal the evidence of their crime, or by people who wanted to hide their wealth from jealous friends or to make an offering to the gods. If archeologists discover a treasure hoard, it is sometimes difficult for them to tell why this treasure was hidden.

Gold encrusted with stones

BURIED GOLD
Roman writers made fun of the Celts because they loved to wear so much ostentatious gold jewelry. And here is the evidence. These neck rings, or torcs, were worn by British Celts in about 75 BCE. Metal threads were wound together to make spectacular, heavy bands in gold, silver, and bronze. Torcs were symbols of high social rank. This buried treasure was excavated at Snettisham in Norfolk, England, between 1948 and 1973. It included more than 70 whole torcs and many other pieces. Why was the Snettisham hoard buried? We may never know.

Roman god Bacchus resting a foot on his panther

Roman god Oceanus with his beard of seaweed

CLOAKED IN MYSTERY
In 1837 two villagers came across a treasure hoard of gold, silver, and jewelry dating back to the 4th century near Pietroasele, Romania. It included a cup, a bowl used for offerings to the gods, a tray, a ring, and necklaces. This is one of four fibulae (brooches used to fasten cloaks) that were found in the hoard. Who buried this hoard and why remain a mystery.

Musician playing for dancers

THE MILDENHALL HOARD
This plate was one of 34 pieces of Roman silverwork that was plowed up from a field in Mildenhall in Suffolk, England, in 1942. The hoard included plates, dishes, spoons, and wine goblets dating from around 350 CE. It seems they were imported into Roman Britain from north Africa and buried during troubled times. Some experts think the hoard is not an ancient burial, but may have been looted in north Africa during World War II (1939–45) and taken back to Britain.

FAR FROM HOME
This bronze statue of the Buddha was made in northern India in the 6th century CE. In 1954, it turned up far from its home, in a Viking treasure hoard on the island of Ekerö, in Lake Mälaren, Sweden. The Vikings' restless journeying, trading, and raiding meant that their treasures came from far and wide.

UNDER THE SOIL
Most treasure hoards are buried in shallow pits and may be accidentally uncovered during plowing. Gold or silver may survive underground, but wood generally rots away, except when preserved in a bog. Buried metal objects can be located with metal detectors, which are a valuable tool for archeologists and popular with amateurs. However, without proper training and supervision, enthusiasts may accidentally damage a site. There is also the risk that a treasure hoard may be removed illegally, destroying valuable evidence of why it was buried.

Crumpled crucifix

ANGLO-SAXON SPLENDOR
In 2009, the largest known Anglo-Saxon hoard was found in a field in Staffordshire, England. It comprised more than 1,500 items, many of silver and gold. Helmet decorations and gem-studded sword parts suggest that the treasure was military in origin. The hoard also included crucifixes. It may have been war booty brought to the area by a raid on a neighboring kingdom.

7th-century gold and silver hoard

Lost cities

Makers of movies and comics love to show adventurous explorers battling through jungles, deserts, and snake pits to discover treasure in lost cities. Lost cities really did exist. Some of them were buried without trace until they were uncovered by archeologists. Others were cities whose ruins local people knew well, but that had escaped the attention of the wider world. How did these cities disappear in the first place? Some may have been abandoned when the environment changed, leaving the inhabitants without water or crops. Others may have been destroyed by floods, war, or disease. However, although the people left and the streets and temples were deserted, their treasure often remained.

DANCING GIRL
This girl dancer is still posing after 4,500 years. She was modeled in bronze in Mohenjo-Daro, a city in the Indus Valley, now in Pakistan. The city was abandoned in about 1900 BCE, perhaps when the Indus River changed course, and remained undiscovered until 1922.

Long, narrow gorge leads to the Treasury at Petra

QUEEN OF THE SUN
Is this the head of Nefertiti, the queen of Egypt? The painted quartzite captures timeless beauty. This treasure is said to have been found at el-Amarna, on the banks of the Nile River. It was here that Nefertiti's husband, the pharaoh Akhenaten, built a new city about 3,350 years ago. He started a new religion based on Sun worship. After his death, the old religion returned. The royal city of the Sun was abandoned. Later, most of its buildings were demolished.

PETRA'S TREASURES
Petra is hidden in a desert valley in Jordan. Its buildings are carved directly from the red sandstone rock face, which is why it is sometimes called the Rose-red City. The Treasury (right) is so called because of legendary claims that treasure is hidden there. The site's real treasures include bronze and terra-cotta figures, mosaics, lamps, and coins. Petra was occupied by the Nabataeans from 312 BCE, who grew rich from trade in Asian spices. Later, under Roman rule, trade declined, and a series of earthquakes buried many buildings under sand.

UNDER THE VOLCANO

In 79 CE a volcano called Vesuvius erupted in Italy. It buried the city of Pompeii in deep ash and triggered a boiling mud slide, which swamped the nearby port of Herculaneum. Thousands died. Memories of the towns faded, but in the 1700s treasure hunters started digging, followed by archeologists. Many Roman marvels were revealed, including statues, wall paintings, pottery, glass, jewelry, mosaics, armor, and coins.

Nature soon takes over ruined cities

ROOTED IN STONE

The city of Angkor Thom and the temple of Angkor Wat in Cambodia date from the Khmer Empire of the 1100s. In 1431, invading armies brought the golden age of Angkor to an end. Soon dense tropical creepers covered most of the city. When French naturalist Henri Mouhot arrived here in 1860, he began the long work of hacking back the vegetation and restoring the fine stone carvings.

OUTPOST OF THE INCAS

In 1911 in Peru, an American archeologist named Dr. Hiram Bingham discovered a site that was overgrown with forest. It was the Incan city of Machu Picchu, high in the Andes Mountains. This city had been an outpost of the Incas, defeated by Spanish invaders in 1532. When the forests were cleared, farming terraces, stone temples, and houses were revealed. The treasures found include silver, gold, musical instruments, and pottery.

Sunken treasure

BENEATH THE WAVES there is another world, where sunlight and shadow give way to the darkness of the ocean depths. Littering the ocean floor are the broken timbers or rusting hulls of shipwrecks sunk to the bottom over the ages. They may have been scattered by storms, or buried under mud and sand, but treasures such as Roman vases, Spanish gold, or bullion from World War II (1939–45) still survive in these watery graves. Across the centuries, fortune seekers have tried to reach wrecks in search of treasure, but only in recent times has technology made it possible to locate and explore the more difficult and remote sites. Marine archeologists can give fascinating insights into the past by exploring these ocean-floor time capsules—if the evidence is not destroyed by treasure hunters.

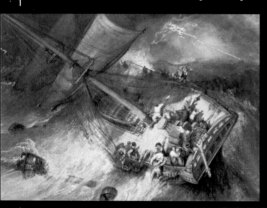

SHIPWRECK!
Ships may be wrecked by storms, by bad navigation—crashing into rocks, sandbanks, or icebergs—or by battles at sea. Most wrecks are located in shallow waters, where there are more navigational hazards. Even today, with weather forecasts, radio, sonar, and satellite navigation, ships still sometimes come to a bad end, along with their valuable cargoes.

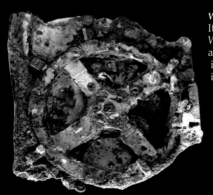

WHAT IS THIS?
It looks like broken clockwork. When Greek divers discovered a wreck off Antikythera island in 1901, they were far more impressed by the statues they raised. But this machine really is remarkable. It was used to calculate the positions of the stars and planets more than 2,100 years ago. Was this the world's first computer?

ARMADA RUBIES
In 1588, Spain's war fleet, the Armada, set out to invade England. It was defeated in the English Channel, and its surviving ships were then scattered by gales as they rounded Scotland and Ireland. Many were wrecked, including the *Girona*. In the 1960s, divers raised 12,000 items from this one vessel, including coins, gold rings, and jewelry.

Gold salamander pendant set with rubies

FACING THE FISHES

This proud statue gazing out over the seabed is one of many treasures discovered beneath the waters of the large harbor at Alexandria, Egypt—a city founded by the Macedonian conqueror Alexander the Great in 332 BCE. The government of Egypt plans to create an underwater museum at the site and has returned many of the artifacts to their watery home.

LIVERPOOL & AUSTRALIAN NAVIGATION COMPANY.
Steam from Liverpool to Australia,
UNDER 60 DAYS.

THE MAGNIFICENT STEAM CLIPPER
"ROYAL CHARTER,"

MELBOURNE, PORT PHILIP,

AUSTRALIAN GOLD

In 1859, the *Royal Charter* sailed from Melbourne, Australia, bound for the English port of Liverpool. The ship carried more than $1.5 million worth of gold, and many passengers also carried personal fortunes made from the goldfields of Australia. The ship was almost home when it was caught by a hurricane and wrecked off the coast of Wales. The gold was scattered in the waves, and 459 lives were lost.

Unbroken china from the Titanic *on the ocean floor*

LOST LINER

It was an iceberg that sank a luxury liner called the *Titanic* in 1912, drowning 1,517 passengers and crew. The wreck was not located until 1985, in the deep waters of the north Atlantic Ocean. Although some passengers were carrying precious rings and diamonds at the time, this was no treasure ship. Even so, its fame ensures that any items from the wreck, even its nuts and bolts, are worth a fortune.

Metal diving helmet from the 1900s

SALVAGE

Even in ancient times, attempts were made to salvage and recover valuable cargo or vessels. However, diving at great depth is very dangerous, because water pressure can damage the human body. Between the 1700s and 1900s heavy diving suits were used, which protected the diver's body. Advances in technology make it easier to explore the seabed today (see pages 48–49).

Spanish treasure fleets

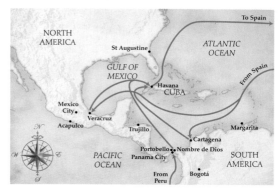

FROM THE SPANISH MAIN
The Spanish shipped treasure out of the ports of Veracruz, Nombre de Dios, and Portobello. The combined fleet of up to 40 vessels would assemble off the coast of Cuba before crossing the Atlantic for Spanish ports. Other treasure routes followed the Pacific coast of South America, and from the 1570s linked Acapulco in Mexico with the distant Philippines in Southeast Asia.

AFTER THE EXPLORER CHRISTOPHER COLUMBUS first sailed from Europe and discovered the Americas in 1492, Spain won control of large areas of this "New World." The Spanish-ruled mainland became known to mariners as the Spanish Main, and soon that term was also applied to the surrounding seas and islands. The Spanish shipped back to Europe plunder from the conquered Aztec and Inca empires, as well as emeralds and silver from the mines of South America. As early as 1521, these treasure ships came under attack from Spain's enemies, and from pirates. In the 1540s, the Spanish decided to group their galleons into heavily armed convoys for protection. These fleets sailed twice each year, laden with precious cargo—jewelry, gold coins, and bullion.

HURRICANE!
In September 1622, a galleon called *Nuestra Señora de Atocha* (Our Lady of Atocha) was caught in a hurricane off the Florida Keys (now in the US) and driven onto a coral reef. Five other ships were also wrecked. They were part of a 28-vessel convoy with a cargo of gold, silver, copper, pearls, and emeralds.

LOST AND FOUND
The wreck of *Nuestra Señora de Atocha* was lost until 1985, when this American treasure hunting team finally located the site. Although some of the treasure had been scattered by the currents, the team recovered a rich haul. But who owned the treasure? The US government claimed that it did, but in the end it was the treasure hunters who won the legal battle.

Gun carriage

Barrel of cast bronze

FIREPOWER
The job of the galleon *Nuestra Señora de Atocha* was to guard the rear of the treasure convoy from attack. There were more than 80 troops on board, and the ship was armed with 20 cannon like this one. Some of the original guns were raised from the wreck when it was discovered.

Cannon from Nuestra Señora de Atocha

COLOMBIAN EMERALDS

Thousands of emeralds have been found at the *Atocha* site, scattered across the ocean floor. Historians believe that this ship alone was carrying about 65 lb (30 kg) of uncut emeralds. Many others were already cut, polished, and mounted in rich gold settings. Most of the emeralds came from the Muzo and Chivor mines in Colombia. These and other mines were seized by the Spanish invaders from 1536 onward. Huge numbers of fine-quality gems were shipped back to Europe.

Emerald and gold pendant

Ornamental falcon

Emerald ring

Emerald and gold cross

Emerald and gold triple ring

SILVER AND MORE SILVER

These beautiful silver boxes fit one inside another. They were made in South America and engraved with designs in the traditional style of Incan silversmiths. They form part of the treasure recovered from the wreck of *Nuestra Señora de Atocha*. These five were protected by a sixth outer box, which was damaged by the pounding of the waves.

HAIL MARY

This little bronze figure of the Virgin Mary with baby Jesus was recovered from the wreck of the *Santa Margarita*, a sister ship of the *Atocha*, which also went down off Florida in the hurricane of 1622. In addition to soldiers and sailors, the treasure fleets carried all kinds of passengers between Spain and the New World. They included priests, officials, and nobles.

Assay marks may show foundry, serial number, purity, and tax paid

BARS OF GOLD

Ingots were assayed (officially stamped to confirm their weight and authenticity) before being exported from Spain's American colonies. This helped to prevent fraud or theft. These gold bars were found in the wreck of the *Santa Margarita*. The loss of this treasure fleet was a major blow to the Spanish economy.

Invaders and raiders

TREASURE CAN AROUSE POWERFUL FEELINGS of greed and envy. Throughout history it has been the cause of robbery and fighting, of quarrels, plots, and secrecy. Bands of armed raiders have attacked ports, towns, monasteries, and temples to seize their riches. Invading armies have pillaged the lands they marched through and carried their booty back home. Generals have recruited soldiers by offering them the chance of plunder and quick riches. In many ancient empires, conquered peoples were required to send their most precious goods to the emperor each year, as tribute. In the 1800s, when European countries ruled many lands overseas, ancient sites were pillaged and their treasures sent back to museums in Berlin, Paris, and London.

FACE OF THE RAIDER?
This gold mask was found in Mycenae, Greece, in 1876. It was thought to show the warrior-king Agamemnon, who raided Troy during the Trojan War (c.1200 BCE). The mask is actually 300 years older, and the face is probably that of another warlike raider.

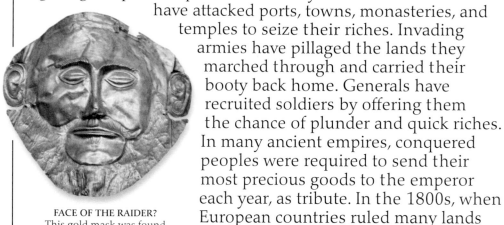

DACIAN GOLD
The ancient region of Dacia (modern Romania) was famous for its gold. When the Romans attacked Dacia between 85 and 106 CE, they won control of the gold mines. The Dacian king, Decebalus, had cunningly buried a huge treasure hoard beneath a river that he had diverted for that purpose, but the Romans learned of this hiding place and seized the treasure.

Warrior sacrificing a ram to the gods of war

TREASURES FROM THE TEMPLE
This frieze is carved in stone on the Arch of Titus in Rome. It commemorates the sacking of Jerusalem by the Romans in 70 CE, when they looted and burned the Second Temple of the Jews. The scene shows the triumph (victory parade) of Emperor Titus. Roman soldiers carry one of the Temple's most holy treasures, the menorah—a golden, seven-branched candlestick sacred to Judaism.

Menorah

Banner describes the treasure to onlookers

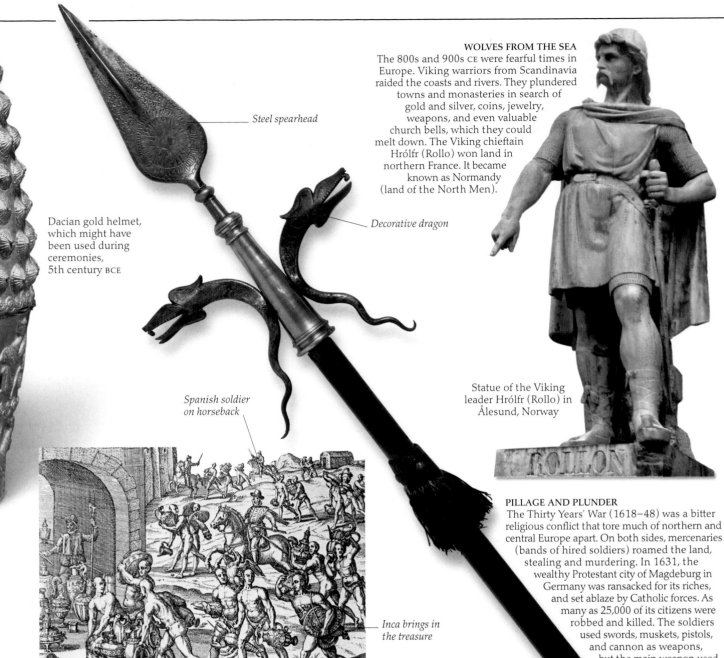

Steel spearhead

Dacian gold helmet, which might have been used during ceremonies, 5th century BCE

Decorative dragon

WOLVES FROM THE SEA

The 800s and 900s CE were fearful times in Europe. Viking warriors from Scandinavia raided the coasts and rivers. They plundered towns and monasteries in search of gold and silver, coins, jewelry, weapons, and even valuable church bells, which they could melt down. The Viking chieftain Hrólfr (Rollo) won land in northern France. It became known as Normandy (land of the North Men).

Spanish soldier on horseback

Statue of the Viking leader Hrólfr (Rollo) in Ålesund, Norway

PILLAGE AND PLUNDER

The Thirty Years' War (1618–48) was a bitter religious conflict that tore much of northern and central Europe apart. On both sides, mercenaries (bands of hired soldiers) roamed the land, stealing and murdering. In 1631, the wealthy Protestant city of Magdeburg in Germany was ransacked for its riches, and set ablaze by Catholic forces. As many as 25,000 of its citizens were robbed and killed. The soldiers used swords, muskets, pistols, and cannon as weapons, but the main weapon used by the infantry (foot soldiers) was the pike.

Inca brings in the treasure

AN EMPEROR'S RANSOM

In 1532, the Spanish invaded the Inca Empire of Peru and captured the emperor Ataw Wallpa. He offered them riches on a lavish scale, in return for his life. He had a large room filled once with gold and twice with silver. The Spanish took the treasure, but then they accused him of treachery, and in 1533 had him garrotted (executed by being strangled).

Pike, infantry weapon of the 1630s

Long wooden shaft

STOLEN HORSES

These powerful horses are made of bronze and date back to the 4th century BCE. The four horses were originally attached to a _quadriga_, or racing chariot. They were once the pride of Constantinople (now Istanbul), capital of the Byzantine Empire. In 1204, Venetian troops looted the horses and in 1254 they were placed in front of St. Mark's Basilica in Venice. In 1797, Napoleon seized them and took them away to Paris, France. The horses were returned to Venice in 1815, and they remain there to this day.

Pirates and buccaneers

PISTOL TERROR
This pirate pistol used during the 1600s and 1700s could terrify the captains of Spanish treasure ships, wealthy passengers, or other pirates in tavern brawls. Fiction paints a romantic picture of pirates. In real life, many were brutal murderers and bullies.

Sparks from the flint, placed here, set off the gunpowder

PIRACY HAS EXISTED as long as there has been shipping. Pirates are sea robbers who prey on ships in search of precious cargo. They steal almost anything of value, but jewels and coins of gold and silver make ideal booty. These are easily carried off, divided up, and sold, and always remain valuable. Only a few pirates became very rich. Many were killed in fights or caught and hanged. Others wasted their wealth or lost it in shipwrecks. Treasure maps and buried chests of pirate gold are largely the invention of storytellers, but the cannonballs, the skull-and-crossbones flags, and the treasure itself were all very real.

BARBARY PIRATES
Pirates from North Africa's Barbary coast raided ships from the 1500s to the 1800s. The most feared were the two Barbarossa ("red beard") brothers, Oruç and Hayreddin. In 1504, Oruç captured two heavily laden treasure galleys belonging to Pope Julius II off the island of Elba.

Ornate dagger in a gold-plated sheath

Largest silver coin is the piece of eight

PIRATE LOOT
From the 1500s to the 1700s, Spanish galleons carried gold and silver in the form of bars and coins from Central and South America back to Europe. These included silver coins worth eight reals, which became known as pieces of eight, and gold coins worth 32 reals, which were called doubloons.

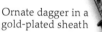

Largest gold coin weighed about 1 oz (28 g)

Gold and silver coins

Diamond and amethyst necklace

DEAD MEN'S CHESTS
Legend has it that Captain William Kidd, who was hanged for piracy in London, England, in 1701, buried many treasure chests. Some of his treasures hidden on Gardiner's Island, New York, were recovered at the time. But the rest? No one knows. Sites all down the coast of North America have been searched ever since—in vain.

FANCY WEAPONS
Pirates would steal ornate swords and daggers from naval officers and rich merchant captains. They might then wear the weapons themselves, in order to show off, or sell them for a good price. But for everyday hand-to-hand fighting, the pirate's weapon of choice was a cutlass—a short, plain, but deadly slashing sword.

A BOOK FOR BUCCANEERS
From the 1630s, Spanish treasure fleets came under attack from buccaneers, a group of outlaws and fugitives who had settled on some Caribbean islands. They lived by hunting, raiding, and piracy. In 1681, a buccaneer named Bartholomew Sharp seized a useful prize from the Spanish—a waggoner, or book of charts, used to navigate the coasts of Central America.

Avery's ship
Fancy attacking
another ship

Henry
Avery's
flag

MOGUL HAUL

In 1695 Henry Avery, also known as Long Ben, launched a savage attack on two ships called the *Fateh Muhammad* and the *Gang-i-Sawai*. They belonged to the Mogul emperor Aurangzeb, who ruled most of India at that time. The pirates looted 500,000 silver and gold pieces, as well as priceless jewels. Avery retired from piracy, but is said to have been cheated out of his fortune. He died penniless.

PIRACY TODAY

Piracy began to decline in the 19th century as the navies of different nations grew stronger, but it still exists in some parts of the world. Many big oil tankers have been hijacked in recent years by armed pirates who demand money from the owners for the ships' safe return. Luxury yachts are targeted by pirates in Southeast Asia and the Caribbean. Here we see Somali suspected pirates, on a small, fast boat, surrendering to a US Navy vessel in the Gulf of Aden.

Points of
the compass

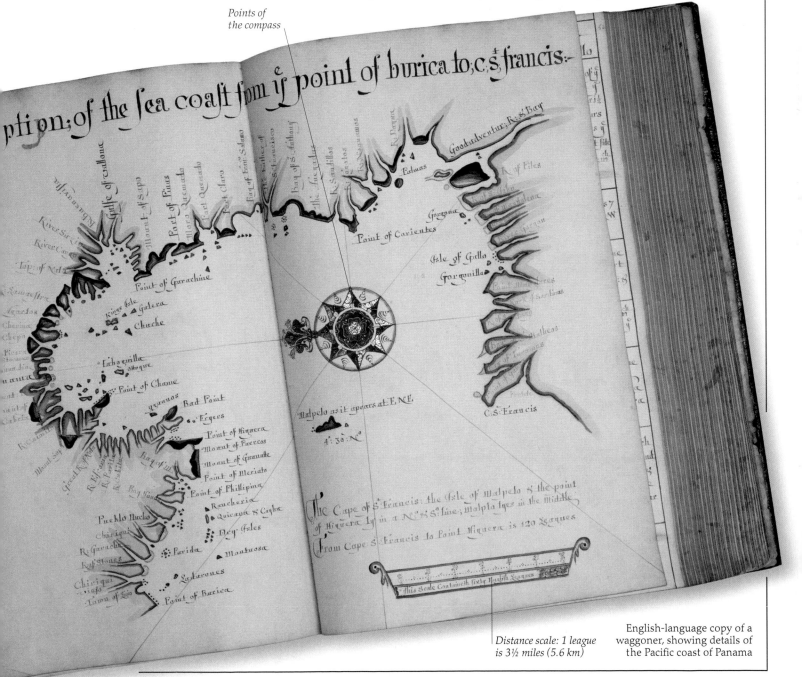

Distance scale: 1 league is 3½ miles (5.6 km)

English-language copy of a waggoner, showing details of the Pacific coast of Panama

Grave robbers

W**HILE PIRATES AND RAIDERS** rob the living, grave robbers steal from the dead. The wonderful treasures placed in tombs as grave goods were stolen even in ancient times. People wanted the wealth so much that they would risk the curses of the gods, the anger of the dead person's descendants, armed guards, and collapsing passages or tunnels. Modern tomb raiders may be poor people desperate to make a little money, amateur treasure hunters, or organized criminals possibly hired by unscrupulous collectors and galleries.

TOMB DETECTIVES
This document tells of an official inquiry into tomb robberies, held in the Egyptian city of Thebes around 1100 BCE. Grave robbing might have been carried out by the tomb's original builders, or even by crooked priests. The punishment for grave robbing was to be impaled alive on a stake. Even so, most tombs discovered in Egypt had been raided for their treasure at some point in history.

Treasures from Ecuador plundered by *huaqueros*

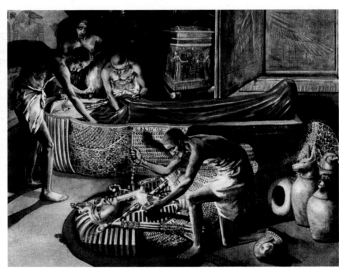

GRASPING FOR GOLD

At first the Egyptians buried their rulers inside huge pyramids, but these highly visible tombs were often robbed. Later, pharaohs were buried in the Valley of the Kings, to the west of Thebes. Their tombs were sealed in underground chambers, with hidden entrances, secret shafts, dead ends, and pitfalls. The valley was heavily guarded—but still robbers broke in. This illustration shows a gang in ancient Egypt stripping a royal tomb of its treasures.

Terra-cotta archer

Hand once held a bow

GUARDING THE DEAD

Qin Shi Huangdi was the first emperor to unite China. He decided to protect his tomb with an army of more than 8,000 soldiers. These were actually life-size statues made of painted terra-cotta (fired clay). When he died in 210 BCE, they were buried around him, on guard for eternity. However, the tomb was raided by a real army within five years of his death.

Vase for kumis, a drink made from mare's milk

Scene shows wild horses being tamed

Pattern of birds and acanthus leaves

BURIED ALIVE

This silver vase dates from about 350 BCE. It was found in 1862, in a Scythian burial mound at Chertomlyk, Ukraine. The grave goods, which included jewelry, gold, crowns, and harnesses, had been scattered and ransacked. Under a pile of rafters, archeologists found the body of a grave robber from long ago, trapped when the roof collapsed on his head.

THE DAMAGE DONE

An Iraqi looter seizes pottery from Ishan Bakhriyat, site of the ancient city of Isin. Years of hard work by archeologists were undone by armed raiders during the invasion of Iraq in 2003. Illegal excavation of tombs means that finds are not properly recorded in position, resulting in the loss of vital information about past civilizations.

LOOTED RICHES

In Italy, grave robbers called *tombaroli* loot ancient Etruscan tombs. In the US, amateur treasure hunters raid Native-American burial sites. In South America, gangs known as *huaqueros* excavate Incan burial sites and sell their plunder to dealers. The looting and smuggling of treasure is a major problem worldwide. Many gold objects that are too difficult to trade may simply be melted down for their value and lost forever.

Quest for El Dorado

New cacique, or ruler

AFTER CONQUERING THE EMPIRES of the Aztecs in Mexico and the Incas in Peru, in the 1500s, Spanish adventurers called conquistadores heard rumors of an even richer land in South America, ruled by a king named El Dorado, "the Golden One." Soon, explorers began calling the land itself El Dorado. For nearly 100 years, explorers obsessed with finding this land battled through dense rain forest and sailed up long rivers. They fought hostile tribes and quarreled with one another, dying of tropical diseases or festering wounds—all for an empty dream of treasure.

REALMS OF MYSTERY
The quest for El Dorado was centered upon the countries we know today as Venezuela and Colombia, around the Orinoco River basin. These lands were still largely unknown to Europeans. There was gold here, but nothing like the wealth of the Incas in Peru. So how had the rumors started?

RUMORS OF A KING
This gold model was made by the Muisca people of Colombia, and it shows their chief, or king, on a raft. It seems that before the Spanish conquest, the throne was usually inherited by the nephew of the previous king. The new king would be taken to the middle of a lake called Guatavita, where he would make offerings of gold and emeralds to the gods. Rumors of this lavish ceremony soon spread far and wide.

Gold dust is blown over the resin-covered body of the king

THE MAN OF GOLD
Tales about the Muisca king, or "Golden One," reached Europe and became even more exaggerated. Some claimed that he bathed in the lake each day, covered in gold dust from head to toe. This fanciful reconstruction of the ceremony was first published by a Flemish printmaker named Theodorus de Bry in 1590.

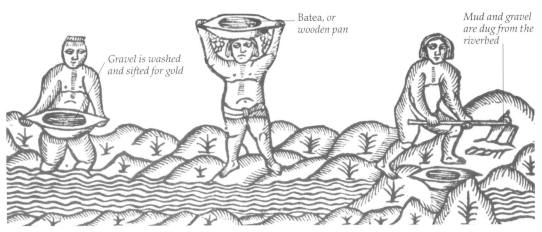

PANNING FOR GOLD

Gravel is washed and sifted for gold

Batea, or wooden pan

Mud and gravel are dug from the riverbed

This engraving from the 1500s shows Native Americans panning for gold in a river. They would collect sand and gravel in pans, add water, then shake the pans to separate the heavy gold from the other materials. The conquest of South America provided the Spanish with ship loads of gold, silver, and emeralds for hundreds of years. The area around Lake Guatavita, however, was not rich in gold, and the rulers must have imported their gold from other regions.

FORTUNE SEEKERS

Among those who joined the doomed quest for El Dorado were many ruthless and violent adventurers from Spain, Germany, and England. A treacherous and cruel conquistador named Lope de Aguirre joined an expedition in 1560. His character was played by the actor Klaus Kinski (above) in the 1972 film *Aguirre, the Wrath of God*.

Priest accompanies the new ruler

THE MAN WHO LOST HIS HEAD

In 1595 English explorer Sir Walter Raleigh reached the Orinoco River west of Colombia. He heard rumors that El Dorado was really even farther west, in the Guiana Highlands. Raleigh returned to England and was imprisoned by the king in 1603, for his supposed involvement in a treason plot. He was only released in 1617, in order to search for El Dorado again. He found no golden land and was executed on his return.

One of the oarsmen, the smallest figures on the edges of the raft

TO THE SACRED LAKE

The first El Dorado expedition was organized in 1529, by a family of German bankers named Welser. Ten years later, conquistadores finally reached Lake Guatavita (above). They found no evidence of ceremonies, no Golden One. Surely, this could not be El Dorado? The search moved elsewhere. In 1580, attempts were made to drain the lake. Since then, treasure seekers have found some gold and silver, but no fabulous riches.

Muisca raft, made of high-grade gold with silver and copper alloy in 1200–1500

Treasure seekers

DURING THE 1700S AND 1800S, the wealthy people of Europe became fascinated by the ancient past. Rich young men went off to see the ruins of ancient Greece and Rome, on what became known as the Grand Tour. It became fashionable for kings and queens to decorate their palaces and gardens with Greek and Roman statues. They ordered ancient sites to be pillaged and their treasures brought back to them. At this time, European nations were very powerful, ruling large overseas empires. They competed with one another to bring back ancient treasures from Asia, Africa, and Pacific Islands. These treasures were put on display in big museums in cities such as Berlin, Paris, and London. Scholars studied the objects and eventually carried out excavations in a more methodical, scientific way. This was the beginning of modern archeology.

SMASH AND GRAB
The lost Roman city of Herculaneum (see page 29) was rediscovered in 1594. In the 1700s, teams of treasure hunters began to excavate the site, looking for statues and gold to adorn royal palaces in Austria and Spain. An engineer named Rocque de Alcubierre dug tunnels and shafts through the 65 ft (20 m) of soil that had covered the site for so many centuries, smashing through precious walls and ancient buildings. This engraving from 1759 shows workers hauling treasures away.

Horsemen form part of a procession in honor of the Greek goddess Athena

A section from the western frieze of the Parthenon

Hieroglyphs, as found on many ancient Egyptian treasures

Demotic script, the everyday language of ancient Egypt

Greek script, which was the key to cracking the code of the other two

KEY TO PAST TREASURES
A French army officer discovered this stone at Rosetta (el-Rashid, Egypt) in 1799. It dated back to 196 BCE and shows the same text written in three different scripts. By comparing them, scholars were able to work out the meaning of hieroglyphs, the mysterious picture writing of ancient Egypt.

BIG BELZONI
Born in Italy, Giovanni Belzoni (1778–1823) was a giant of a man who first made his name as a circus strongman, as seen here on stage in London. In 1814, he went to Egypt and was employed to excavate ancient treasures and ship them back to Britain. He often damaged the sites, but did make important discoveries. These inspired a growing fascination for all things Egyptian. Belzoni exhibited his finds at the Egyptian Hall in London's Piccadilly.

Statue of a winged bull is lowered onto wooden rollers by ropes

HAULED AWAY
Between 1845 and 1851 an archeologist named Austen Henry Layard carried out excavations at Kalhu (Nimrud) in Assyria, northern Iraq. Here he is shown removing a statue from an Assyrian palace. More than 2,700 years old and weighing 11 tons (10 metric tons), the statue was floated down the Tigris River by raft and then shipped to the British Museum.

THE PARTHENON SCULPTURES
These riders and galloping horses carved in marble seem to come alive. They formed part of a frieze (ornamental band) that decorated all four sides of the Parthenon, the great temple of Athens, Greece, from 438 BCE. In the 1800s, a British ambassador named Lord Elgin was given permission by the city's Turkish rulers to remove many sections and take them back to Britain. They are now exhibited in the British Museum, but the Greek government wants the carvings returned to their original home.

Coral headdress represented in brass

Facial markings were part of a ritual

ROYAL ELEGANCE
This graceful head of Idia, the queen mother, comes from the royal court of Benin, Nigeria. It is made of brass and dates from the 1500s. In 1897 British troops seized more than 1,000 treasures from Benin's royal palace. Many were exhibited in museums and collections, revealing the glory of African arts and crafts. There are calls for these treasures to be returned to their homeland.

SERIOUS STUDY
By the 1880s, archeologists such as William Matthew Flinders Petrie (1853–1942) sought historical knowledge, not only treasure and profit, from ancient sites. Petrie was fascinated by archeology as a young boy and went on to survey the Great Pyramid at Giza and many other sites.

Archeology in action

ATTITUDES TO THE DISCOVERY OF TREASURE began to change during the 1800s and the 1900s. There was a growing interest in studying the objects in order to understand the societies that had created them. The old "smash and grab" approach was replaced by careful excavation, meticulous recording, and research—the scientific process we call archeology. The first archeologists came mostly from European countries, but soon there were new generations of local scholars working on sites in Egypt, China, Iraq, India, and the Americas. Archeology has been transformed in recent years by scientific advances and methods of dating materials. They bring us much closer to the world of our ancestors and their most treasured possessions.

TELLTALE OUTLINES
Archeologists can learn a great deal by going up in the air as well as underground. Aerial photographs often reveal burial chambers, earthworks, field boundaries, or building outlines. This is Tara, once the seat of the high kings of Ireland. From this angle, the circular earthworks with a central mound, and the ditch and bank around them, are clearly visible.

HISTORY DETECTIVES
Archeologists work beneath the floor of St. Blaise's Church in Dubrovnik, Croatia, in search of the building's origins. Three churches were built at this spot. The first church was built here in the 500s or 600s. It was rebuilt later in the Middle Ages and yet again after 1667. The church's treasury includes reliquaries (containers for storing relics, such as the bones of a saint), gold plates and basins, and paintings.

Scraper

Paintbrush

Tweezers

Dental pick

Toothbrush

Tools used for excavating small, delicate objects

AT THE DIG
Archeologists may need to dig down through various layers, or strata, in the soil, each left by a different period of human settlement. The archeologist's toolkit on site includes fine picks and brushes (above), trowels, sieves, tape measures, a plumb line (a weighted string to line up objects vertically), and a ranging pole (to show the scale of objects on camera).

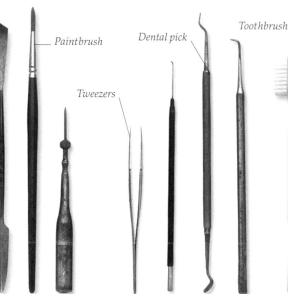

Microscope for close examination

Black figure work on red terra-cotta

CAREFUL, NOW!
A gentle brushing away of the soil reveals an Etruscan vase at Montalto di Castro, Italy. The recovery of each item of treasure and its safe treatment, storage, and care is essential. It is also important not to damage the site as a whole when removing treasure. The use of remote cameras and endoscopy (imaging through a flexible tube) allows burial chambers or caves to be explored with little demolition or damage.

EVERY DETAIL COUNTS
Whether the site is under water or on dry land, the position of every item discovered in a particular area must be recorded within a measured grid. Its vertical position within the strata of soil or sediment must also be noted. Every item found must be measured, cataloged, and, where possible, identified. The work is very slow and painstaking. If the rules are broken by untrained treasure hunters, precious information will be lost.

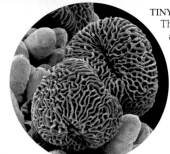

TINY CLUES
This is a tiny speck of pollen from a plant, seen under the microscope. By identifying pollen found with treasure, experts may be able to find out where the treasure originated, which crops were grown in that region, or what the climate was like long ago.

Case made of layers of linen or papyrus and covered with plaster

SCANNING A MUMMY
The painted coffin case of a 2,800-year-old Egyptian mummy is placed in a CAT scanner, like the ones used in hospitals. The body inside belonged to a priestess named Tjentmutengebtiu. The 3-D X-ray images revealed details of her body and teeth, without breaking open the coffin or unwrapping the mummy.

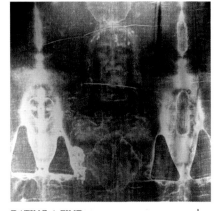

DATING A FIND
Is this the face of Jesus Christ imprinted on a shroud in Turin, Italy? Some believe it is, but radiocarbon tests in 1988 suggested the cloth was made 1,300 years after Jesus Christ lived. Dating of material is based on chemistry, magnetism, radioactivity, or wood growth.

Discovery at Saqqara

Gilded wings

GOLDEN IBIS
This golden ibis was found at Saqqara. The ibis was a sacred bird in ancient Egypt, believed to be a form taken by Thoth, the god of learning, and also associated with the genius of Imhotep, the pyramid builder. Thousands of mummified ibises were brought to Saqqara between 332 and 32 BCE. They were left as offerings to the gods.

SAQQARA IS A BROAD AREA of desert to the south of Cairo, Egypt. Kings, queens, and officials were buried here for more than 3,500 years. The first-ever pyramid, an impressive stone monument with stepped sides, was built here. It was raised for the pharaoh Djoser, who died around 2610 BCE. Many mastabas (brick buildings raised over underground tombs) are also found here. For thousands of years, Saqqara's treasures were plundered by robbers. Archeologists have excavated the site ever since the 1850s, when Frenchman Auguste Mariette began to dig here. What treasure could possibly be left to discover? Thanks to the skills of modern archeology, plenty. In 2009, the remains of 30 mummies were discovered in just one burial chamber.

THE PYRAMID BUILDER
Imhotep (c. 2650–2600 BCE) is the world's first architect, engineer, and doctor to be known by name. He built the great stepped pyramid at Saqqara and was chancelor to the pharaoh Djoser. He is shown here in the classic pose of a *sesh,* or official. This bronze figure was made more than 2,000 years after his death, by which time he was revered as a god of wisdom.

THE BEADED MUMMY

In 2005, a team of Australian and Egyptian archeologists was exploring a 4,200-year-old tomb at Saqqara when they stumbled across some finds dating from about 2,500 years ago. These included a well-preserved mummy covered in a net of beads made from faience—a glazed ceramic containing quartz sand. The beaded mummy was found inside a cedarwood coffin.

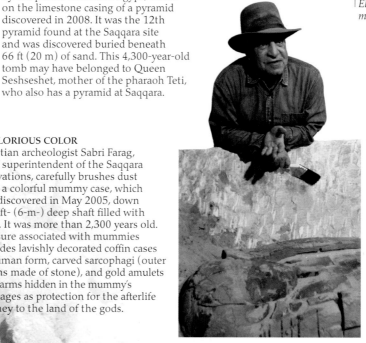

Facial features represented in beads

Elaborate collar made of beads

Well-preserved inscriptions

SYMBOLS OF THE PAST

An archeologist carefully cleans hieroglyphs (picture symbols used by the priests of ancient Egypt) found on the limestone casing of a pyramid discovered in 2008. It was the 12th pyramid found at the Saqqara site and was discovered buried beneath 66 ft (20 m) of sand. This 4,300-year-old tomb may have belonged to Queen Seshseshet, mother of the pharaoh Teti, who also has a pyramid at Saqqara.

Wooden outer coffin

IN GLORIOUS COLOR

Egyptian archeologist Sabri Farag, chief superintendent of the Saqqara excavations, carefully brushes dust from a colorful mummy case, which was discovered in May 2005, down a 20-ft- (6-m-) deep shaft filled with sand. It was more than 2,300 years old. Treasure associated with mummies includes lavishly decorated coffin cases in human form, carved sarcophagi (outer coffins made of stone), and gold amulets or charms hidden in the mummy's bandages as protection for the afterlife journey to the land of the gods.

A SYSTEMATIC APPROACH

Archeologists, including the head of Egypt's Supreme Council of Antiquities, Zahi Hawass, are meticulously investigating the tomb of the 30 mummies discovered in 2009. Archeology at Saqqara is as complicated as any detective story. Mummies may be more recent than the tomb in which they are buried. Pyramids may have crumbled away or been hidden by desert sands. Only a methodical approach can reveal the truth.

Pyramid of Djoser

Pulley to lower archeologists into the burial chamber 36 ft (11 m) below

A NEW DISCOVERY

New discoveries in Egypt attract great international interest, so archeologists must deal with the present world as well as the past. It is important that the public is informed about new finds and is inspired by them, but at the same time the site and the new discoveries must be protected from harm. When news spread about the discovery of 30 mummies in 2009, journalists and site workers gathered outside the burial chamber for updates on the finds.

Searching the seabed

TREASURES FOUND ON the ocean floor need as much care in their recovery as those excavated from fields or tombs. Archeologists use many of the same tools under water as they do on land, but a suction dredge must be used to clear mud and sand from the seabed. The invention of scuba (Self-Contained Underwater Breathing Apparatus) in the 1940s made it possible for divers to stay under water using their own air supply, rather than an airline to the surface. The use of waterproof cameras and remote imaging also made locating and recording marine treasure easier. Disadvantages for marine archeologists include poor visibility, cold, sickness from water pressure, and communication difficulties.

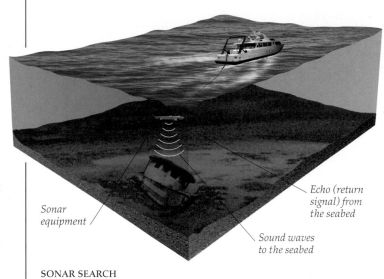

Sonar equipment

Echo (return signal) from the seabed

Sound waves to the seabed

SONAR SEARCH
It is possible to search the seabed for shipwrecks or treasure using sonar (SOund Navigation And Ranging). This equipment, mounted on the exploration ship or towed after it, sends out pulses of sound. It records the time it takes for an echo to return from the objects it meets. These sound patterns are turned into computer images or a paper printout. Some sonar equipment is designed to face straight down onto the seabed, while other types can scan sideways.

DEEP DOWN
A submersible is a small vessel or chamber designed to operate at extreme depths below sea level. Here, a Russian-designed Mir submersible explores the 1912 wreck of the *Titanic* at a depth of 12,536 ft (3,821 m), for filming the US documentary *Ghosts of the Abyss* in 2003.

INVESTIGATING THE WRECK
A diver wearing scuba gear explores the wreck of an Arab ship that sank in 1025 in Serçe Limani Bay, off the Aegean coast of Turkey. The ship contained a cargo of glassware, as well as pottery, coins, weapons, and chess and backgammon pieces. The shipwreck was in 115 ft (35 m) of water, an easy depth for divers to work. However, it was buried under tons of sand, which had to be cleared in order to reach the treasure.

Divider or compass
for measuring
distances on a chart

100-ton
cradle hoist

Navigational
instruments
salvaged from the
Mary Rose

Protractor for
checking the
ship's course
on a chart

Diving mask
allows the diver
to see clearly
under water

SHIVER ME TIMBERS!
In 1982, the timbers of an old English warship were raised
from the bottom of the sea. The *Mary Rose*, the pride of
King Henry VIII's navy, sank in 1545. Items discovered
on board included weapons, armor, lanterns, coins,
dice, and medical equipment. The ship's hull is itself
a treasure to be preserved. This process involves many
years of spraying with water and wax, followed by a
long drying period.

THE PIRATE HAVEN
A newspaper of 1692 reports
the destruction of Port Royal in
Jamaica after an earthquake. Quays
and several streets of houses and stores
sank beneath the waves. The port was
a haven for pirates and rogues, and some
preachers claimed that this disaster was
a punishment from God. From the 1980s
onward, marine archeologists began
exploring the underwater buildings and
found candlesticks, gold and pearl
jewelry, silver forks and spoons,
porcelain, and weapons.

Medieval
amphora
(pottery jar)

Square grid is used
to map out the site

THE *BATAVIA* STORY
Drunkenness, murder, and plans to steal 250,000 silver
coins followed the shipwreck of the *Batavia* off Western
Australia in 1629. The ship's owners, the Dutch East
India Company, restored order among the survivors and
salvaged some silver. The wreck was rediscovered in
1963, and an archeological survey began in 1972. The
ship shown above is a modern replica of the *Batavia*.

Time capsules

ARCHEOLOGISTS MAY UNCOVER gold, silver, jewels, and treasure worth a fortune. However, the real value of their finds is something far more precious—a glimpse into a past world. Each archeological site is a time capsule. Muddy trenches and dusty tombs offer much more than burials and bones, or chests full of shiny metal. They tell us how real people lived long ago. The information collected by archeologists can be joined up with other sources—books and journals, old paintings, histories, and official records of birth, death, imprisonment, shipping, or taxes. Putting together this great jigsaw puzzle can bring the past to life.

TIME TRAVEL
The Roman seaside town of Herculaneum (see page 29) is a good example of an archeological time capsule. It was frozen at one moment in time, buried during the eruption of Vesuvius in 79 CE. It was remarkably well preserved, so that today we can walk through its streets and see its homes, stores, public baths, mosaics, wall paintings, boathouses, and fountains.

Fine inlays of red limestone, lapis lazuli, shell, and bone

Jasper ring

LADY OF THE RINGS
This treasure tells a tragic story. The skeleton was found on what had been the beach at Herculaneum. It belongs to a woman who may have been trying to escape from the town by boat. She wore two rings, which can be seen here, although how the rings came to be on a bone in her hand rather than on her finger remains a mystery. Close to her body archeologists also found earrings, two solid gold bracelets, and some coins.

IT'S ALL IN THE GAME
This board game was made before 2600 BCE. It was found at Ur, Mesopotamia (Iraq). The board was clearly made by skilled craftworkers, using costly materials. The lapis lazuli inlay shows that Ur's merchants traded with Afghanistan. This find also tells us that a class of rich people lived in Ur, perhaps nobles or rulers, with plenty of time for leisure activities, and that they enjoyed the same kind of games that we play today.

One of seven counters for each player

Chinese bronze bell from c. 1105 CE

Chinese bronze bell from c. 400 BCE

CHINESE CHIMES
What can we learn from these bells? They prove that the ancient Chinese were brilliant metalworkers who also understood a great deal about music. Not only were Chinese bells perfectly tuned, but each bell could also produce two different notes, depending on where it was struck. Today's experts can even reconstruct the sounds of the past with these objects. These two bells were made at very different times, showing how knowledge was passed on from one generation to the next in Chinese civilization.

Engraving depicting an elephant

CLUES FROM A CAULDRON
This panel is from a silver-plated cauldron found at Gundestrup, Denmark. Made after 120 BCE, it depicts gods and warriors from Celtic Europe, but the metal and workmanship suggest it may have originated in southeast Europe or western Asia. Engravings of elephants and mythical animals also offer clues about the exchange of ideas and knowledge in the past.

Page representing February from a book of hours

Peasant warms her feet by the fire

EVERY PICTURE TELLS A STORY
This art treasure is a book of hours (prayer book) made for a French nobleman, Jean, Duc de Berry, in the 15th century. From it we can find out about medieval prayers and religious customs, and also discover how books were made, copied, and illustrated at the time. Its pictures offer us a wealth of historical detail about weather, fuel, farming, animals, transportation, dress, daily life, and architecture.

Ariane 5 rocket that will launch the KEO satellite

INTO OUTER SPACE
The KEO satellite is due to be launched into space in 2010 or 2011. It will return to Earth in about 50,000 years' time, carrying a time capsule from our own age, to be discovered by future human beings or aliens. Inside will be all kinds of items, including a diamond containing human blood and samples of Earth's soil, water, and air. Could these be treasures of the future?

Whose treasure?

TREASURE THAT HAS BEEN FOUND is often called a treasure trove, from the French word *trouver*, meaning "to find." Treasure troves have posed legal problems for centuries. Who should own discovered treasure—the finder, the present landowner, or the nation? If a treasure hoard remains unclaimed by its original owner, who should profit from its discovery? How is treasure defined, and how old does it have to be? The laws vary from one country to another, and sometimes from one region or state to another. In the end, treasure is a public issue, because the historical information it offers and the appreciation of its beauty cannot belong to one person alone. It belongs to all humanity.

WHAT DO WE HAVE HERE?
Members of the public discover all kinds of ancient objects, often using metal detectors, but they may not have a legal right to keep them. Under the law of England and Wales, finds of precious metals, as well as coins more than 300 years old and prehistoric artifacts, must be officially registered. The landowner generally has first rights. Historical items, such as Roman bronze work (above), should be reported to a local official.

FINDERS KEEPERS?
In the US, treasure law varies from one state to another. Generally, the old treasure trove principle of "finders keepers" still applies. However, in Idaho in 1999, two workmen laying a driveway unearthed a jar containing gold coins. In court, the treasure was awarded not to the workmen, but to the landowner.

ENFORCING THE LAW
An Italian policeman checks a rich haul of ancient treasure seized from a dealer in illegal antiquities. Many of these items were looted from tombs of the Etruscan period (800–396 BCE) by gangs of robbers. Treasure laws must be strictly enforced if the plunder of archeological sites is to be stopped. Penalties may include the confiscation of undeclared treasure, heavy fines, or a long jail sentence.

Etruscan and Roman statues and metalwork

Gold head representing
a defeated enemy,
Ashanti, Ghana

Bronze statue
known as the
Lady of Kalymnos

QUITE A CATCH
Greek law states that discovered
treasure belongs to the nation.
To ensure that finds are reported
and not sold secretly, the government
pays finders 10 percent of the treasure's
value. This statue was found by a
fishing crew off the island of Kalymnos
in 1994. The crew was given €440,000
($650,000) for reporting the find.

NATIONS AND CULTURES
This gold head was part of the royal treasure
of the Ashanti Kingdom. It was plundered
by the British army in Ghana in 1874. Such
treasures are often a vital part of the culture
of a nation or people. Their ownership, and
the question of where they should be displayed,
is a matter of fierce debate in our own times.
Should they be returned to the cultures that
originally made them?

Bold decorative
goldwork

WHO OWNS A WRECK?
In 2008, a US marine exploration company found
a shipwreck off the Channel Islands. It was the first
HMS *Victory* (above), which sank in 1744. Today, its
gold cargo may be worth $1 billion. The wreck lies in
international waters, but since the ship was in the
British navy, the United Kingdom claims ownership.
It is discussing a financial deal with the US company.

On show

TREASURES OF THE LOUVRE
As early as the 1190s, a fortress in the center of Paris, the French capital, housed crown jewels, armor, and precious manuscripts. This later became the royal palace of the Louvre and housed the royal art gallery. Today, it is one of the world's most famous museums, and 8.5 million people visit it every year.

SPLENDOR OF ANCIENT GREECE
The Acropolis Museum in Athens opened in 2009. It houses nearly 4,000 precious items, including statues and vases, and offers a panoramic view of the Parthenon temple on top of the city's great rock. The museum hopes that ancient Greek treasures currently held elsewhere, such as sculptures from the Parthenon (see page 42), will one day be exhibited here.

Greek *kraters* (wine-mixing vessels) from 4th-century-BCE Italy

BECAUSE SO MUCH TREASURE was originally designed to dazzle the eye, it can make a fascinating public display. Museums and galleries are modern treasure houses, where the wonders of the past may be marveled at by everyone. Here, the exhibits can be explained and given their place in history. We can learn how beautiful things were made, who made them, and why. Sometimes, museums may exchange items from their own collection with those of other countries or regions for special exhibitions. Museums conduct important research and restore, conserve (preserve from damage and decay), and curate (look after) precious items. They may also run educational programs for the public.

*Fragment of
an engraved
panel*

*Engraved
steel panel*

*Wet or dry cleaning
may be neccesary*

Original helmet, assembled

Replica of the helmet

HISTORICAL JIGSAW PUZZLE
Reconstruction poses many problems and may be difficult to correct if
a mistake is made. This Anglo-Saxon helmet was found in 1939 in a ship
burial at Sutton Hoo, England. It dates from about 625 CE. The helmet had
collapsed into hundreds of rusty fragments. These were reassembled (left).
When new, the helmet may have looked like the steel replica (right).

CONSERVATION IN ACTION
American conservation experts took a whole year to clean
and repair this 17th-century Italian tapestry, *The Crucifixion*.
Textile conservation combines historical research with
repairs requiring delicate needlework
and the mastery of dyeing techniques.
Textiles are very fragile and may be
damaged by moths, wear and tear,
or daylight, which causes fading.
This work is now back on display
at the Cathedral Church of St. John
the Divine in New York City.

*Hair
remains
preserved*

REST IN PEACE?
This mummified body of an Inca woman from
South America is on display at a German museum.
It is a fascinating exhibit, but there are
growing concerns that removing dead
bodies from their graves and showing
them in museums may offend some
peoples' cultural and religious beliefs.
Australian Aborigines, for example, have
successfully demanded that the remains of
their ancestors be returned from museums
and reburied in their ancestral lands.

THEY NEVER LEFT THEIR POST
The terra-cotta army of the first Chinese emperor, Qin Shi Huangdi (see page 39),
is a moving sight. The model troops still stand on guard, row upon row. They are
displayed in the very place where they were originally buried and later excavated,
outside the Chinese city of Xian. Instead of removing treasures to a distant national
museum, they can sometimes be displayed on site.

KEEPING WATCH
A museum security guard keeps an eye on visitors and exhibits using CCTV (closed-circuit television) cameras. Technology has made it easier to protect treasure 24 hours a day.

Safe and sound

MANY EXCITING MOVIES have been based upon heists, or attempts at robbery. It is certainly true that as long as treasure exists, people will try to steal it. Moats and cannon once protected the treasures inside palaces and castles. Today's bank vaults, museums, and galleries are protected by security guards, laser beams, and all kinds of electronic equipment. Some treasures are so valuable that they cannot be insured or replaced. Museums have to guard against vandalism and destruction by floods or fire. Items of treasure can also be damaged if the air is too moist or too dry, or if there is too much bright light. Some caves with prehistoric paintings have had to be closed because the breath of visitors was damaging the ancient pigments.

Engraving of Thomas Blood (second from left) fleeing the Tower of London with the crown jewels

COLONEL BLOOD
In 1671, Colonel Thomas Blood and his gang tried to steal the English crown jewels from the Tower of London. They made off with the crown, filed a scepter in two, and Blood stuffed an orb down his breeches. Blood was caught during the escape and imprisoned, but was later pardoned by the king.

Two of the damaged vases from the Chinese Qing dynasty

THEFT OF THE *MONA LISA*
The world's most famous painting is Leonardo da Vinci's *Mona Lisa* (or *La Gioconda*), painted more than 500 years ago. In 1911, it was stolen from the Louvre museum in Paris by an employee who hid in a broom cupboard. In 1956, one visitor threw acid at it, and another visitor hurled a rock. The painting survived and is protected in a climate-controlled, bulletproof casing.

ON GUARD
This robot has been designed to patrol a gallery and guard its treasures. Modern electronic surveillance equipment in museums can monitor movement and light and triggers alarms if there are intruders.

Enamel painting of flowers and foliage with gilded highlights

THE HEIST THAT FAILED
The Millennium Star diamond was the centerpiece of celebrations for the year 2000 at London's Millennium Dome. A gang planned to steal the diamond, but was secretly observed by police, who swapped the real diamond for a fake. Smoke bombs, hammers, a bulldozer, and a speedboat were all used in the attempted heist, but the robbers were arrested.

PROTECTION DURING WAR
US troops patrol Baghdad's National Museum during the Iraq War. Considerable damage was done to the museum's treasures by looters at the start of the war in 2003. Wartime authorities generally try to remove precious exhibits to secret stores in remote places, to prevent bomb damage and looting. Protection of outdoor monuments and remote archeological sites is often even harder to enforce.

WHOOPS!
Accidents will happen. In 2006, a visitor to the Fitzwilliam Museum in Cambridge, England, tripped over his own shoelaces, fell downstairs, and smashed three precious Qing dynasty vases from 17th-century China. The museum authorities had to map where each of the pieces fell and painstakingly reassemble them. The vases had been viewed by 9 million previous visitors without any problem.

One of more than 400 pottery shards that had to be reassembled

Fakes and forgeries

WHEN GENUINE TREASURE is worth huge sums of money, it is not surprising that many people try to pass off fakes, or forgeries, as the real thing. Deceptions have been carried out for as long as treasure has existed. Worthless metals have been passed off as gold, or glass as diamonds. In the Middle Ages, fake Christian relics such as pieces of the cross or bones of saints were sold as the real thing. Today, the market in fake antiquities is worth billions, despite the fact that methods used for detecting forgeries have never been better. Textiles, canvas, and pigment can be dated accurately. Pottery and paintings can be X-rayed. Metals can be analyzed. Computers can store large amounts of data to be quickly accessed so that genuine finds, sales, and other records can be compared.

THE MUMMY WHO NEVER WAS
Photographers jostle for pictures of a mummy at Pakistan's National Museum in Karachi in 2000. Some experts claimed that this mummy was of a Persian princess from around 600 BCE. However, radiocarbon dating indicated that the coffin and the body were very recent. This was a fake, which had been put on sale on the black market with an asking price of $11 million.

Painted areas stay black during firing

Vase turns red when air is introduced during firing

Forged black figure-ware vase, 20th century CE

POTTERY PUZZLE
The Greek vase on the left was made in Athens in the 6th century BCE. The red and black colors were made by varying the supply of oxygen during firing. The modern vase on the right was made by just the same method. A process called thermoluminescence dating can now be used to confirm exactly when a piece of pottery was fired. It measures the amount of radiation absorbed since the

PUTTING ON THE STYLE

Tom Keating (1918–84) was an English art restorer who faked paintings in the style of old masters. He produced about 2,000 such works. They convinced many people, but he was no forger. He deliberately left clues in each painting indicating that it was a fake. He sometimes used modern canvases or wrote "This is a fake" in lead-based paint so experts would be able to tell that the painting was not genuine. His goal was to show just how corrupt and clueless the art market could be.

CAN YOU SEE THROUGH THIS ONE?

This crystal skull was bought by the British Museum in 1897 and was believed to be a 500-year-old Aztec treasure. However, when experts examined it under an electron microscope, they had their doubts. The quartz crystal came from Brazil, not Mexico, and seemed to have been cut and ground with machinery unknown to the Aztecs. The Smithsonian Institution in the US owns a similar skull, and it may also be a fake.

THE AGE OF THE WOLF

The Romans claimed that their state was founded by twins, Romulus and Remus, who were abandoned as babies and kept alive by a she-wolf who gave them her milk. A famous bronze statue of this wolf was widely believed to date from the 5th century BCE. But perhaps not. Radiocarbon and thermoluminescence dating technology now suggests that this wolf was probably made in the 13th century CE, with the twins added in the 15th century.

IS THE LADY A FRAUD?

For many years experts believed this Dutch painting of a young woman playing a virginal (a kind of harpsichord) was the work of master forger Han van Meegeren (1889–1947). X-rays and infrared light revealed that the pigment and canvas were from the 1600s, suggesting it really is the work of the great artist Johannes Vermeer (1632–75).

Still undiscovered

THE SEARCH FOR LOST TREASURE is never ending. It is fueled by rumors and tall tales, and by the sensational claims often made in popular books and movies. Even if a treasure existed in the first place, it may have been recovered long ago, or may be lost forever. Sometimes lost shipwrecks may be found using new technologies or traced through records of cargoes and shipping. On land, careful archeological detective work brings the best results. Even so, many discoveries are accidental or based on guesswork. Sad to say, old myths and legends or folklore rarely lead to the discovery of treasure. However, everyone thought that the Trojan War was no more than a story, until the great German archeologist Heinrich Schliemann claimed to have located the site of Troy in Turkey in the 1870s.

The story of the Ark is common to Christian, Jewish, and Muslim faiths. This "Torah crown" is for holding Jewish scriptures

Picture of the sacred Ark of the Covenant

PIRATE TREASURE
The hunt for pirate treasure has led people to scour the coasts and islands where pirates hid out in the 1700s. Edward Teach, better known as Blackbeard (c. 1680–1718), is said to have buried treasure around Caribbean and west Atlantic shores before he was killed. His ship, the *Queen Anne's Revenge*, has been located, but intensive searches have yet to find buried treasure chests.

Treasure chest

LOST IN THE WASH
In 1216, King John of England was traveling through the marshy lands around the Wash, a broad inlet of the North Sea. His packhorses and wagons were caught by the incoming tide, and lost in the sea and mud. They were carrying the king's baggage and, many believe, the crown jewels. The location of this disaster, however, is uncertain, and rivers have changed their courses since the Middle Ages. Despite several searches, no treasure has been found.

THE AMBER ROOM

Imagine a great hall, lined with panels of the finest amber. Such a room was crafted in the German kingdom of Prussia about 300 years ago. In 1716, the amber panels were presented to the Russian royal family. They were eventually assembled, redesigned, and enlarged to adorn a large hall at the Catherine Palace, near St. Petersburg, Russia. In 1941, during World War II, German invaders dismantled the panels and sent them home, but this precious cargo was lost during the war, and its whereabouts remain a mystery. A reconstructed Amber Room now stands at the Catherine Palace.

A detail from the reconstructed Amber Room

The original Amber Room in the 1930s

TREASURE OF THE TEMPLARS

The Templars were a powerful and rich religious order of Christian knights in Europe who fought in the Crusades (religious wars in the 12th and 13th centuries). Some said they even possessed the golden Ark of the Covenant from the Temple of Jerusalem, which contained holy relics. In 1307 King Philip IV of France tried to destroy the Templar order and claim their wealth. It was said that several ships carrying their most precious treasures escaped from France. But to where? The destination of the fleet and the treasure are debated to this day.

THE TIGER'S GOLD

During World War II (1939–45), Japanese troops invaded Southeast Asia, looting large amounts of gold, silver, and jewelry. This treasure ended up with the forces of General Tomoyuki Yamashita (right) nicknamed the "Tiger of Malaya" for his conquest of British colonies in Malaya (now Malaysia) and Singapore. He was said to be shipping the treasure to Japan from the Philippines when the war ended. He surrendered and was executed, but the fate of the treasure remains unknown.

THE QUEEN'S JEWELS

At the beginning of the French Revolution (1789–99), King Louis XVI and his wife Marie-Antoinette (right) arranged for their gold and diamonds to be smuggled out of France on a ship called the *Télémaque*. It was anchored in the Seine River, near Quillebeuf, when a fierce storm started. The ship sank into deep mud. Repeated salvage attempts in the 1800s and 1900s were in vain.

Treasure in the future

OUR INTEREST IN TREASURE is focused on history and the past. It is harder for us to judge what the lasting treasures of our own time are, and even more difficult for us to guess what will be considered valuable in the future. Will distant planets be visited by miners, and will treasure fleets be made up of spacecraft? Perhaps water will become as precious and rare as gold dust. Maybe society will change, so that the world's treasure is shared by all. Or warfare will involve weapons so terrible that treasures and ancient sites can no longer be protected from destruction. Two things are certain. Human beings will continue to use their ingenuity and skill to make beautiful objects, and people will still treasure the things they consider to be valuable and rare.

TREASURE, OR JUST PAPER?
Money made out of gold has been treasured throughout history. Paper money is different. It is valuable only because a government says so. If its design changes, for instance, the old designs may no longer be accepted as money, and the paper becomes worthless. If you found a stash of money in the attic in only 20 years' time, it might be most valuable as insulation. In 200 years' time, though, the money might be rare and of huge historical value.

A TREASURY OF SEEDS
When seafarers such as the Polynesians traveled to new lands thousands of years ago, they took with them seeds of the crops they cultivated along with their most valued possessions, to ensure they would have food in their new homes. Today, seeds of the world's cultivated crops are collected and stored in huge vaults deep inside a mountainside in the Arctic. These will ensure the future of crop production in the event of a major disaster affecting the global environment. Seeds may prove to be the most precious treasure of all.

Entrance to the seed vault buried 390 ft (120 m) inside a mountain at Svalbard in Spitsbergen, Norway

Decorative panel of steel, mirrors, and prisms reflects light so that it can be seen from far away

Blast-proof, high-security steel door

SPACE TREASURE
The Phoenix Lander spacecraft scoops soil from the surface of the planet Mars in 2008. The systematic mining of distant planets, moons, or asteroids for their precious minerals and metals is still a long way off, but it has been imagined by science-fiction writers and film-makers for many years. If there were intergalactic treasure fleets, might they be attacked by space pirates?

HERE'S TO THE YEAR 3000!
The *New York Times* celebrated the year 2000 by preparing a millennium time capsule. It contained all kinds of everyday items, including sound recordings, books, and parts of computers. This legacy was assembled as a gift to archeologists of the future. The capsule, housed at the American Museum of Natural History in New York City, is meant to be opened in the year 3000.

5-ft- (1.5-m-) high stainless-steel time capsule sculpted by Spanish engineer Santiago Calatrava

TODAY'S TREASURE, TOMORROW'S JUNK?
Today, all kinds of electronic gadgets and gizmos are treasured items. They are admired for their appearance and also for their performance. While such items are costly, they are often abandoned as soon as the public is persuaded to buy something even more clever and smart. Only a few items become classics, valued in the long term for their innovation and design. Perhaps this iPod will become a treasure of the future?

MEDICINE AND KNOWLEDGE
Medicine may not be everyone's idea of treasure, yet emperors of ancient China sent expeditions to scour the world for life-saving potions and elixirs. Edward Teach, the pirate known as Blackbeard (see page 60), carried off a medicine chest for his ship, the *Queen Anne's Revenge*. Medicines can save lives and protect us from old and new diseases. They are a product of human knowledge and of ideas passed on through the ages. As new diseases enter the world, perhaps it is this knowledge that will become the true treasure.

Timeline of treasure

THROUGHOUT HISTORY, HUMANS in every part of the world have produced the most beautiful treasures, whether made of gold, silver, jewels, rich cloth, carved wood, porcelain, glass, or ivory. Treasures have been hidden and hoarded in troubled times, or looted by raiders, invaders, or pirates. As treasure hunting gave way to archeology, museums replaced palaces as the great treasure houses of the world. Now, we can all see treasures our ancestors could only dream of.

Relief plaque from the silver cauldron found at Gundestrup, Denmark

BCE (Before Common Era)

c. 73,000
Shell necklaces with red ocher coloring are made in South Africa, as discovered at Blombos Cave in the 1990s.

c. 38,000
Use of red pigment at Carpenter's Gap, Australia, suggests early Aboriginal art.

c. 23,000
One of the first realistic representations of a woman's face is carved in ivory in Brassempouy, France.

c. 15,000
Scenes of wild animals being hunted are painted on rock in a cave in Altamira, Spain, using charcoal and ocher.

c. 12,000
Small figurines of a sitting woman and a thinking man—masterpieces of Stone Age art—are made in Cernavoda, Romania.

c. 6000
Metallurgy—extracting metals from rocks and working them into tools and weapons—begins in western Asia. People value worked metals as treasure.

c. 4600–4200
Lavish gold and copper ornaments and pottery are buried in hundreds of graves in Varna, Bulgaria.

c. 2635–2610
First step pyramid is built over the tomb of the pharaoh Djoser in Saqqara, Egypt.

c. 2600
Grave of Puabi, a queen or priestess of Ur, Mesopotamia (Iraq), is furnished with a splendid gold headdress, jewelry, a lyre, and a chariot.

c. 2500
Bronze figurine of a dancing girl is made in Mohenjo-Daro, Pakistan.

Statue of gold, lapis lazuli, and shells made between 2600 and 2400 BCE in Ur, Iraq

c. 2000
Phoenicians from the eastern Mediterranean begin trading in silver, copper, tin, glass, textiles, dyes, and precious wood.

c. 2000–1350
Knossos Palace in Greece is the center of the Minoan civilization. Palace treasures include silver, copper, bronze, jewelry, paintings, and pottery.

c. 1350
Mycenaean warriors and rulers of northern Greece are buried in beehive-shaped graves along with gold masks, armor, and jeweled weapons.

1324
Tutankhamun, the boy pharaoh, is buried in Thebes, Egypt, and his tomb is filled with treasure, including gold masks, collars, and pendants.

c. 1300
Fine bronze model of a wagon hauling the Sun across the sky is made, perhaps as an offering to the gods, in Trundholm, Denmark.

883–612
Assyrian palaces at Nineveh, Dur-Sharrukin (Khorsabad), and Kalhu (Nimrud) in Mesopotamia (Iraq), become known for their crowns, ivory, jewelry, cedar wood, glazed brickwork, and carved stone.

c. 800–300
Etruscan tombs in Cerveteri, Italy, are filled with treasures of fine statues, carved stone, pottery, and bronzes.

c. 640
First metal coins are minted in Lydia (Turkey).

626–539
Beautiful tiles, glazed bricks, jewelry, bronze, and terra-cotta are produced during the second Babylonian Empire of Mesopotamia (Iraq).

c. 550
Rhytons (drinking horns) of silver and gold are produced during the Achaemenid Empire in Persia (Iran). Other treasures include carved stone, glazed bricks, and coins.

c. 438
Parthenon temple with a 39-ft- (12-m-) high ivory and gold statue of the goddess Athena is built in Athens, Greece.

312
Nabataeans build the rock-hewn city of Petra, Jordan. Noted treasures include bronze work, terra-cotta artifacts, lamps, and coins.

c. 300
World's earliest surviving knotted carpet is made in the Pazyryk valley, Altai Mountains, Siberia.

210
China's first emperor, Qin Shi Huangdi, is buried with an army of terra-cotta statues near Xian, China.

c. 120
Silver cauldron embossed with scenes from Celtic mythology is made. It is found in Gundestrup, Denmark, in 1891.

113
Prince Liu Sheng and Princess Dou Wan from Mancheng, Hebei province, China, are buried in jade suits.

c. 75
Gold torcs (neck bands) are made by the Celts of Britain. A hoard, or possibly a votive offering, of gold torcs is found in Snettisham, England, between 1948 and 1973.

CE (Common Era)

70
Roman army under Titus sacks Jerusalem and loots treasures from its sacred temple.

79
Mount Vesuvius near Naples, Italy, erupts and buries the Roman towns of Pompeii and Herculaneum, with all their treasures.

c. 100
Some 20,000 gold ornaments, also jewelry of lapis lazuli and turquoise, are buried in six graves at Tillya Tepe, near Sheberghan, Afghanistan.

c. 100
Buddhist cave temples are hewn from rock and decorated with masterpieces of painting and sculpture at Ajanta, Maharashtra, India.

c. 500
Monumental Buddhist shrine, the Shwedagon pagoda, is built and ornamented with gold and jewels in Yangon, Myanmar.

c. 625
Anglo-Saxon ship is buried with two noblewomen along with a helmet, shield, purse, cauldrons, silver bowls, clasps, buckles, and silverware in Sutton Hoo, England.

c. 700
Silver chalice decorated with gold, brass, pewter, and enamel is made in Ardagh, Ireland.

c. 800
The Book of Kells is created, possibly on the British island of Iona. Its pages are beautifully illustrated and decorated with illuminated letters.

c. 850–1200s
Exquisite bronze figures of Hindu gods are produced during the reign of the Chola dynasty in south India.

860s
Gold coins and jewelry are raided or traded by the Vikings. A magnificent hoard of gold coins and jewelry is found in Hon, Norway, in 1834.

c. 1000
Human sacrifices and votive offerings of gold, silver, jade, and obsidian are thrown into a pool in the Mayan city of Chichén Itzá, Mexico.

c. 1100
The Khmer people of Cambodia build Angkor Thom city and temples famed for their remarkable stone carvings.

1204
Italian city-state of Venice sacks Constantinople (Istanbul) and loots its gold, silver, ivory, altars, icons (holy pictures), thrones, and tapestries.

c. 1300
Chimú Empire of Peru, with its capital at Chan Chan, produces fine gold, silver, copper, and bronze work, and elaborate pottery.

c. 1440
Benin Empire in Nigeria, west Africa, produces magnificent heads and figurines in bronze, ivory, and iron.

1501–1736
Safavid Empire in Persia (Iran) produces beautiful tiles, carpets, pottery, textiles, manuscripts, calligraphy, and miniature paintings.

1504
The pirate Oruç, one of the Barbarossa brothers, captures the pope's treasure ships off the island of Elba in Italy. The Barbary (Berber) coast of north Africa becomes notorious for piracy.

1521
Spanish invaders conquer and plunder the Aztec Empire of Mexico. Treasures include gold, silver, textiles, feather work, and jewelry.

1529
Start of a search for a legendary land of gold, known as El Dorado, believed to be in Venezuela or Colombia, South America.

1532
Spanish invaders loot the temples and treasuries of the Inca Empire in Peru.

1622
Spanish fleet carrying treasure from South America to Spain is wrecked off the Florida Keys, a group of low islands now in the US.

1629
Dutch ship *Batavia* carrying a fortune in silver is wrecked off the western coast of Australia.

1668
Buccaneers commanded by the privateer Henry Morgan attack the Spanish colony of Portobello, netting a fortune in looted treasure and ransom money.

1695
Pirate Henry Avery ("Long Ben") attacks and loots treasure from the ships of India's Mogul emperor Aurangzeb.

1700s
Akan people of west Africa, such as the Ashanti, produce gold jewelry and weights used for the gold trade, made of copper, brass, and bronze.

Akan gold ring with star motif from Ghana, Africa

1701
Captain Kidd is hanged for piracy in London. Piracy in the Caribbean, north Atlantic, Gulf of Guinea, and Indian Ocean reaches a high point.

Silk cloth, with a design of a young man holding a cup and flask, from the Safavid dynasty, 17th century, Persia (Iran)

Apple blossom egg made by Peter Carl Fabergé

1709
Excavations at Herculaneum, and later at Pompeii, trigger a new fascination with the treasures of ancient Rome.

1798
French invade Egypt, taking with them 167 scholars, including historians and scientists. They survey many monuments, inspiring a great interest in Egypt's ancient treasures.

1871
Archeologist Heinrich Schliemann discovers golden headdresses, jewelry, and drinking vessels from the probable site of ancient Troy at Hissarlik, Turkey.

1885
Jeweler Peter Carl Fabergé makes Easter eggs of gold and jewels for the Russian royal family.

1888
Cowboys discover the site of Mesa Verde, Colorado, inspiring new interest in archeology and treasure hunting at Native-American sites in the US.

1911
US archeologist Hiram Bingham uncovers a lost city of the Incas at Machu Picchu, Peru.

1922
English archeologist Howard Carter discovers the treasure of Tutankhamun in the Valley of the Kings in Thebes, Egypt.

1968
Lavish grave goods of an Iron Age chieftain are discovered at Hochdorf, Germany.

1978
Grave of the Lord of Sipán in northern Peru is excavated. Grave goods, including jewelry, headdresses, gold, and silver, are recovered.

1985
The wreck of the Spanish treasure ship *Nuestra Señora de Atocha* is located off Florida.

2003
Archeological sites are damaged and ancient treasures looted during the war in Iraq.

2009
The largest hoard of Anglo-Saxon treasure, containing about 1,500 gold and silver objects, is discovered by Terry Herbert in a field in Staffordshire, England.

Treasure map of the world

THIS MAP SHOWS the discovery sites of some of the fantastic treasures buried, sunk, hoarded, discovered, or displayed around the world over the ages. These beautiful objects discovered were made by skilled craftspeople and they can reveal a great deal about the history, culture, and values of people through time.

NORTH AMERICA

NORTH ATLANTIC OCEAN

MESA VERDE, CO (SITE 1)
Beautiful pottery is part of the southwest Native-American tradition in the US. This pot found in Mesa Verde was made by the Acoma from the neighboring state of New Mexico. It shows that the cultures traded with one another.

SOUTH AMERICA

PACIFIC OCEAN

SOUTH ATLANTIC OCEAN

SIPÁN, PERU (SITE 5)
This gold, copper, and turquoise crown made by a Moche craftsman around 1,500 years ago was among the many treasures found in the tomb of the "Lord of Sipán" in northern Peru.

TREASURE SITES

1 Mesa Verde, CO Native-American Anasazi dwelling (see map)

2 Chichén Itzá, Mexico Maya and Toltec city (see p. 24)

3 Florida Keys Wrecks of the Spanish treasure fleet (see pp. 32–33)

4 Port Royal, Jamaica Port and city drowned in an earthquake (see p. 49)

5 Sipán, Peru Lord of Sipán burial, Moche culture (see p. 22)

6 Machu Picchu, Peru Lost city of the Incas (see p. 29)

7 Benin Kingdom, Nigeria Ivory, brass, and iron figures (see pp. 14, 16, 43)

8 Nok, Nigeria Terra-cotta figures, Nok civilization (see map)

9 Valley of the Kings, Egypt Tombs of the pharaohs (see pp. 6, 22, 39)

10 Saqqara, Egypt Burial ground and site of first pyramid (see pp. 46–47)

11 Delphi, Greece Religious site with surviving ruins (see p. 25)

12 Pompeii and Herculaneum, Italy Roman towns buried by the eruption of Vesuvius (see pp. 29, 42, 50)

13 Hochdorf, Germany Burial site of a Celtic chieftain (see p. 23)

14 Brassempouy, France Mammoth ivory carving of a woman, referred to as "Venus" (see p. 8)

15 Altamira, Spain 17,000-year-old cave paintings (see p. 20)

16 Ardagh, Ireland Celtic Christian chalice (see p. 19)

17 Sutton Hoo, England Anglo-Saxon ship burial (see p. 55)

18 Oseberg, Norway Viking ship burial (see p. 23)

19 Gundestrup, Denmark Silver cauldron in Celtic style (see p. 51)

20 Chertomlyk, Ukraine Scythian burial mound (see p. 39)

21 Pietroasele, Romania Mysterious 4th-century treasure hoard (see p. 26)

22 Varna, Bulgaria Burial site with gold grave goods (see p. 10)

23 Lydia, Turkey Anatolian kingdom that minted the world's first coins (see p. 10)

24 Petra, Jordan Nabataean desert city (see p. 28)

25 Ur, Iraq Mesopotamian city-state, burials with treasure (see p. 23)

26 Kalhu (Nimrud), Iraq Assyrian capital on the Tigris River (see p. 43)

27 Ecbatana (Hamadan), Iran Ancient city of the Median, Parthian, and Persian empires (see p. 10)

28 Tillya Tepe, Afghanistan Burial with gold ornaments in both eastern and western styles (see p. 23)

29 Indus Valley, Pakistan Cities of Mohenjo-Daro and Harappa, abandoned in 1900 BCE (see p. 28)

30 Tirupati, India Sacred Hindu site—temples include Venkateswara (see p. 19)

31 Zaraysk, Russia Prehistoric site occupied by mammoth hunters (see p. 8)

32 Pazyryk valley, Russia Scythian burial site, location of the world's earliest knotted carpet (see p. 15)

33 Dunhuang, China Ancient city on the Silk Road with Buddhist cave temples (see p. 20)

34 Xian, China Ancient city near the terra-cotta army tomb (see pp. 39, 55)

35 Mancheng, China Royal burials in suits of jade (see p. 13)

36 Khok Phanom Di, Thailand Stone Age burial site with shell jewelry (see p. 9)

37 Angkor Thom, Cambodia Great city of the Khmer civilization (see p. 29)

38 Kakadu, Australia Center of Aboriginal tradition and ancient rock art (see map)

39 Beacon Island, Australia *Batavia* shipwreck site (see p. 49)

40 Wairau Bar (Te Pokohiwi), New Zealand Māori archeological site (see p. 15)

POMPEII, ITALY (SITE 12)
This Roman jewelry, buried under volcanic ash after the eruption of Vesuvius in 79 CE, remains as beautiful as on the day it was made.

UR, IRAQ (SITE 25)
This splendid ceremonial baton from the Mesopotamian city-state of Ur is decorated with gold. It was found in the royal burial chambers alongside many other magnificent treasures.

EUROPE

AFRICA

ASIA

XIAN, CHINA (SITE 34)
This ghostly model army was discovered near Xian. Made of terra-cotta, the army was designed to guard the tomb of the first Chinese emperor in 210 BCE.

PACIFIC OCEAN

INDUS VALLEY, PAKISTAN (SITE 29)
Figurines, seals, and models were treasures discovered at Indus Valley archeological sites, such as the cities of Mohenjo-Daro and Harappa.

NOK, NIGERIA (SITE 8)
This fine head of a woman was modeled in terra-cotta by a sculptor of the Nok culture, more than 1,800 years ago.

AUSTRALASIA

INDIAN OCEAN

KAKADU, AUSTRALIA (SITE 38)
Australian Aboriginal art, such as this rock painting of a fish, celebrates ancestral spirits, myths, landscapes, and tribal totems (symbols).

SAQQARA, EGYPT (SITE 10)
Many mummies have been excavated at Saqqara, a rich burial ground and archeological site. Important Egyptians buried their dead here over a period of thousands of years.

Find out more

SOMEWHERE NEAR WHERE YOU LIVE, you will find museums, archeological sites, and galleries for people interested in treasure. Treasure does not always mean jewels or precious metals. Everyday objects from the 1800s or 1900s may be just as fascinating as crown jewels. Old photograph albums may not have great value today, but to future generations they may be as significant as the treasure of Tutankhamun. If you are interested in searching for treasure yourself, make sure you learn how to do it according to the approved methods of archeologists. Listen to advice, be patient, take great care, report any finds, and enjoy the search!

TREASURED MEMORIES

Items that bring back memories are known as memorabilia. These *Titanic*-related memorabilia were discovered in a shoebox belonging to Lillian Asplund (1906–2006), a survivor of the sinking of the *Titanic* (see page 31). They are not valuable in themselves, but are a form of treasure because of their association with the tragedy of the *Titanic*. You too could search your home for rare and valuable memorabilia that someone in your family may have collected.

VISIT A MUSEUM

This shining armor from the reign of King Henry VIII of England (1509–47) is on display at the Tower of London. Viewing treasure in a museum allows you to find out more about the treasure itself and the period of history it came from. Many museums also have learning centers or organize special projects and activities for students.

BE AN EYEWITNESS

The best way to experience an ancient palace, a lost city, or a place of treasure is to visit the archeological site itself. A century ago, the ruins of Machu Picchu (below) in Peru were very difficult to reach because of the thick vegetation that surrounded them. The site is now easy to access and is a stunning place to visit. Nearer to home, look for other archeological sites that are easy to reach.

Huayna Picchu rises 1,200 ft (365 m) above Machu Picchu

Face to face with the past at Machu Picchu, Peru

USEFUL WEBSITES

- News and information related to metal detector-based treasure hunting: **www.treasurehunting.com**
- Latest news from the Archaeological Institute of America: **www.archaeology.org**
- Official site of geocaching, a high-tech treasure-hunting game played by families and adventurers throughout the world: **www.geocaching.com**
- An introduction to archeology: **www.archaeology.mrdonn.org**
- News and information about archeology, with interesting links: **www.bbc.co.uk/history/archaeology**
- Portal to shipwreck and treasure sites: **www.seasky.org/links/sealink10.html**
- Website on pirates and treasure: **www.history.com/content/pirates**
- The online home of *dig*, the archeology magazine for kids: **www.digonsite.com**
- The US National Park Service's website on archeology is full of information for budding archeologists: **www.nps.gov/archeology/PUBLIC/ kids/index.htm**
- The Discovery Channel's Pompeii website, featuring a web-only documentary about the city's final day: **dsc.discovery.com/convergence/ pompeii/pompeii.html**

Cracked flint stone

HANDS ON!

Serious treasure hunting means getting a handle on archeology. In many countries and regions, there are archeology clubs and activities that are lots of fun and an ideal stepping stone to later archeological studies. This student from Rzeszów University in Poland is uncovering the past at a 40,000-year-old Neanderthal campsite in Kietrz, Poland. The Neanderthals formed a branch of the human family that died out about 30,000 years ago.

Places to visit

Rijksmuseum, Amsterdam, the Netherlands

METROPOLITAN MUSEUM OF ART, NEW YORK, NY
The Met boasts an unparalleled collection of historical treasures, from ancient Egyptian statues to priceless Chinese porcelain. The Met's uptown branch, the Cloisters, is also worth checking out for its incredible collection of medieval artifacts, including the famous Unicorn Tapestries.

FIELD MUSEUM, CHICAGO, IL
At the Field Museum's Grainger Hall of Gems, visitors can see an amazing array of precious jewelry, both ancient and modern, including many pieces shown at the 1893 World's Columbian Exposition.

LOS ANGELES COUNTY MUSEUM OF ART, LOS ANGELES, CA
With a huge variety of artworks and decorative objects from the ancient world to today, LACMA is a superb destination for anyone interested in treasure. The world-renowned Costume and Textiles collection is especially impressive.

NATIONAL MUSEUM OF NATURAL HISTORY, WASHINGTON, DC
Operated by the Smithsonian Institution, this museum's Mineral Sciences collection gives visitors a chance to see an amazing array of precious stones and jewelry, including the breathtaking and world-famous Hope Diamond.

WHYDAH MUSEUM, PROVINCETOWN, MA
In 1717, the pirate ship *Whydah* sank off the coast of Massachusetts. Today, visitors can see some of the treasures rescued from the wreck. See www.piratesexhibit.com for details.

BRITISH MUSEUM, LONDON, ENGLAND
The British Museum contains one of the largest collections of treasure in the world, from ancient Greek sculptures to the burial objects of an early British king.

RIJKSMUSEUM, AMSTERDAM, THE NETHERLANDS
Exhibits of fine art, gold, silver, ceramics, jewelry, and costumes.

Lore and legend

THE HUMAN FASCINATION with treasure has very deep roots. Treasure formed part of the myths of ancient Greece and was lovingly described in the epic tales of the Middle Ages. As early as the 1700s, the deeds of pirates were told in ballads. Fairy tales and folklore are full of stories of poor families discovering pots of gold. Today, novels, movies, and television programs return to the same theme—our never-ending dream of treasure.

ARABIAN NIGHTS (OR 1,001 NIGHTS)
A group of medieval tales from Persia, Arabia, and India. Treasure tales include those about Aladdin's cave and Sindbad the Sailor's valley of diamonds.

BEOWULF
An early medieval epic tale about Scandinavian warriors and heroes, and a treasure hoard guarded by a dragon.

CROCK OF GOLD
According to Irish folklore, there is a magic crock (pot) of gold to be found at the end of every rainbow. The catch is, you can never reach it!

CURSE OF TUTANKHAMUN
When the tomb of the young Egyptian pharaoh Tutankhamun was opened in 1922, journalists claimed that an ancient curse would strike down those responsible. When anyone even remotely associated with the site did die, it was blamed on this curse.

DRAGONS
Mythical fire-breathing beasts in Asian and European folklore and mythology. They were often guardians of treasure caves.

EXCALIBUR
The magical sword in the tales of King Arthur, a legendary 6th-century British ruler. It was returned to the Lady of the Lake after his death.

FAIRY GOLD
In Celtic lands, fairies were said to pay people in shining gold, which would turn into leaves and stones the next day.

Jason seizes the Golden Fleece in an illuminated manuscript from c. 1460

FAIRY TALES
Fairy tales from all over the world, such as *Jack and the Beanstalk*, tell of poor people magically receiving or discovering gold.

GOLDEN APPLES
Some European myths tell of golden apples that made anyone who ate them immortal. In Greece, they were said to grow in a magical garden tended by nymphs called the Hesperides.

GOLDEN FLEECE
In Greek myth, this fleece of solid gold came from a magical winged ram. It was given to King Aetes of Colchis (modern Georgia), but seized by the hero Jason and his crew, the Argonauts.

HAZEL WAND
A forked hazel twig that was supposed to be able to detect the presence of buried minerals or treasure.

THE HOBBIT
This 1937 children's book by JRR Tolkien tells of the adventures of the home-loving hobbit Bilbo Baggins and his quest to find a treasure cave guarded by the dragon Smaug.

INDIANA JONES
The hero of a series of adventure films (1981–2008), Jones is an archeologist who battles his enemies to win hoards of treasure.

KING SOLOMON'S MINES
A 19th-century adventure story by Henry Rider Haggard in which the heroes find a hidden African cave full of ivory, diamonds, and gold.

KOH-I-NOOR (MOUNTAIN OF LIGHT)
Once an Indian royal treasure, this diamond has been part of the British crown jewels since 1877. A legend says that its owner will rule the world, but also know all its miseries. Only a woman or a god can wear it without bad luck.

LOST CITIES OF THE TAKLAMAKAN
Large central Asian desert where, it is believed, many cities filled with treasure lie buried.

MIDAS
This legendary king of Phrygia (in Turkey) asked the gods to make everything he touched turn into gold. Unfortunately, that included his food!

The front cover of the 1911 edition of *Treasure Island*

NIBELUNGS
According to German and Norse mythology, a royal family who owned a vast hoard of treasure seized by a hero named Siegfried. It was eventually thrown into the Rhine River.

PEDLAR OF SWAFFHAM
An English folktale about a pedlar who dreams he will find treasure if he stands on London Bridge. A Londoner mocks him and says he will find treasure back home in Swaffham. The pedlar returns home and finds the treasure there.

PIRATES OF THE CARIBBEAN
A series of adventure films about pirates and treasure, begun in 2003, starring Johnny Depp, who plays the pirate Captain Jack Sparrow.

THE THIRTEEN TREASURES
In Welsh legend, a list of 13 magical treasures of the "island of Britain." Among them are a sword, drinking horn, cauldron, chariot, invisible cloak, knife, and chessboard.

TREASURE ISLAND
First published in 1883, this children's adventure story by Robert Louis Stevenson is a classic tale of pirates and buried treasure.

TREASURE OF THE SIERRA MADRE
This 1927 novel by B. Traven was made into a movie in 1948. It tells of a rich discovery of gold in the Mexican desert that leads to jealousy, violence, and murder. In the end, the gold dust blows away across the sands.

WOLFERT WEBBER, OR GOLDEN REAMS
This atmospheric tale about buried treasure is from *Tales of a Traveler*, a collection of short stories and essays written by Washington Irving in 1824.

Glossary

ALLOY
A mixture of two or more metals.

AMPHORA
A pottery container once used in Mediterranean lands for storing wine or oil.

AMULET
A lucky charm, believed to protect the wearer from harm.

ASSAY
To test or certify the metal content of bullion or ore.

BASE METAL
Any nonprecious metal, such as iron or lead.

BOOTY
Plunder; items taken from an enemy during war.

BULLION
Gold or silver in bulk, generally in the form of ingots or bars.

Calligraphy in Arabic script on a decorated tile

BURIAL MOUND
An ancient mound of earth, often with a stone or timber chamber, containing bodies and often grave goods. Also known as a barrow or tumulus.

CALLIGRAPHY
The art of writing in a very fine, beautiful, and decorative way.

CHALICE
A drinking cup, often made of precious metal, especially one used during Christian worship.

CONSERVATION
The protection and care of a precious object or site.

CRUCIBLE
A bowl or a part of a furnace, used in metalworking for smelting ore or melting metals.

DIADEM
A jeweled headband or small crown.

ENAMEL
A colorful glassy finish melted onto the surface of pottery or metal.

FAIENCE
A glassy ceramic popular in ancient Egypt.

GEM
A precious stone or jewel.

GOLD LEAF
A very thin foil made of hammered gold and applied to objects for decoration.

GRAVE GOODS
Items such as jewelry and regalia placed in a tomb with the dead person.

HIEROGLYPHS
A kind of writing with picture symbols used on monuments and in formal documents in ancient Egypt.

HOARD
Gathered treasure or other precious items, often hidden away for use at a later date.

INGOT
Metal molded into a bar.

MEDIEVAL
Relating to the Middle Ages, the period of history from around 450 to 1500 CE.

METAL DETECTOR
An instrument that uses electromagnetism to locate hidden metal.

ORE
Any rock that can be mined for its metal content.

PANNING
Sieving and washing soil, gravel, or sand in a pan, to separate any precious minerals it contains.

PIGMENT
Coloring used to make ink, paint, or dye.

PILLAGE
To steal valuable goods during a raid, an attack, or a war.

PORCELAIN
A form of high-quality, translucent pottery valued in the past for its beauty and rarity.

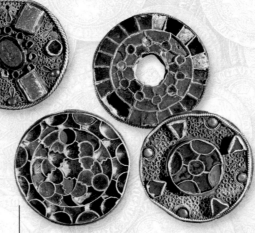

Medieval French silver earrings with filigree (wire work)

Votive offering of a seated female figure from ancient Mesopotamia (Iraq)

PRECIOUS METAL
A valuable metal, such as gold or silver.

REGALIA
The emblems of royalty, such as crowns, scepters, orbs, swords, rings, and robes.

RESTORATION
Returning a precious object or painting to its original condition by repairing any damage.

SALVAGE
The recovery of a cargo or ship after a shipwreck.

SHIP BURIAL
A ceremonial burial inside a ship or in a ship-shaped grave.

SHRINE
A container for holy relics or a holy place of pilgrimage or worship.

SMELT
To fuse or melt ore so that its metal content may be extracted.

STRATUM (pl. STRATA)
A layer of soil or rock belonging to a certain period, for example, in an archeological dig.

TIME CAPSULE
A collection of items that represents or typifies a particular period in time.

TREASURE TROVE
Any treasure that is discovered or, in some situations, a legal definition of treasure.

TREASURY
A storehouse for treasure, money, or other precious or sacred items.

VANDALISM
The careless, ignorant, or deliberate destruction of property or treasured items.

VOTIVE OFFERING
A treasured item offered to a god or gods as part of a vow or religious practice.

Index

A

Acropolis Museum (Athens) 54
amber 9, 13, 61
Amber Room (Catherine Palace) 61
amulets 24, 47
Angkor Thom (Cambodia) 29, 66
Anglo Saxons 27, 55
archeology 43, 44–45, 46–47, 50
Ardagh Chalice 19, 66
Ark of the Covenant 60–61
Australian Aboriginal art 67
Avery, Henry (Long Ben) 37
Aztec Empire 14–15, 32, 40, 59

BC

Barbarossa brothers 36
Batavia (ship) 49, 66
Benin Kingdom 14, 16, 43, 66
Blackbeard (Edward Teach) 60, 63
Blombos Cave (South Africa) 8
Book of hours 51
Book of Kells 20–21
Brassempouy (France) 8, 66
British Museum 42–43, 59
buccaneers 36–37
burial mounds 10, 11, 23, 39
burial suits 13
cannon 32
carpets 15
cathedrals 7, 19
caves 8, 20
Celts 23, 26–27, 51
ceramics 15, 31, 39, 45, 48–49, 54, 56–57, 58, 66
chained libraries 21
chests, treasure 17, 36
Chichén Itzá (Mexico) 24, 66
Chimú people 25
China 9, 13, 14, 15, 17, 20, 39, 50, 55, 66
churches 18–19, 44
coins 6, 10, 36, 49, 52
conservation 55
Constantinople 35
crown jewels 12, 56
crowns 12, 16
currency 62

DE

dating techniques 45, 58, 59
Delphi (Greece) 25, 66
Diamond Sutra 20
diamonds 12, 13, 57
divers 7, 30, 31, 32, 48–49
Djoser, Pharaoh 46
drinking vessels 10–11, 23
Egypt, ancient 6, 14, 22, 24, 28, 31
El Señor, Lord of Sipán 22, 66
El Dorado 40–41
electronic gadgets 63
electronic surveillance 56–57
emeralds 33
Etruscans 39, 45, 52

FG

Fabergé eggs 13, 65
fairytales 70
fakes and forgeries 58–59
feathers 14–15
figurines 9, 28, 33, 67
Florida Keys 32, 66
folklore 70
future treasure 62–63

HI

headdresses 14–15, 16, 18–19
helmets 55
Herculaneum (Italy) 29, 42, 50, 66
hieroglyphs 43, 47
hoards 6, 26–27
Hochdorf (Germany) 23, 66
horses, bronze 35
human sacrifices 24
ibises 46
illumination 20–21
Imhotep 46
Inca Empire 29, 32, 35, 40
Indus Valley (Pakistan) 28, 66, 67
ingots 33, 36
invaders 34–35, 61
ivory 8, 14, 16

JK

jade 9, 12–13
Japan 61
Jerusalem 18, 34
jewelry 6–7, 8–9, 13, 26–27, 30, 33
jewels 12, 13, 33, 61
KEO satellite 51
Khmer Empire 29
Khok Phanom Di (Thailand) 9, 66
Kidd, Captain William 36

LMN

Lady of Kalymnos 53
lost cities 28–29
Louvre (Paris) 54, 56
Lydia (Turkey) 10, 66
Machu Picchu (Peru) 22, 66, 69
Māori 6, 15, 66
marine archeology 7, 30, 48–49
masks 6, 14, 22, 34
Mayan Empire 24
metal detectors 27
metalworking 10, 50
microscopic examination 44, 45
Millennium Star diamond 57
Ming dynasty 15
Moche culture 22, 66
money burning 25
mosaics 17
mummies 45, 46–47, 55, 58, 67
museums
    ancient treasures 42–43, 54–55
    security 56–57
    visiting 68, 69
musical instruments 15, 23
myths 70
Native Americans 39, 66
Nefertiti, Queen 28
New World 32
Nigeria 14, 16, 43, 66

OPQ

offerings, religious 24–25
Orinoco River 40, 41
Oseberg (Norway) 23, 66
paintings 20–21, 59
Parthenon sculptures 42–43, 54
Pazyryk Valley (Russia) 15, 66
pearls 12

Peru 6, 22, 25, 29
Petra (Jordan) 28–29, 66
pigments 20–21, 58, 59
pillage and plunder 35
pirates 36–37, 60
Pompeii (Italy) 29, 66
pottery, see ceramics
pyramids 39, 46, 47
Queen Anne's Revenge (ship) 60, 63

R

raiders 34–35
regalia 16–17
relics 7, 44, 58
rock art 20, 67
Romans 7, 13, 26, 27, 29, 42, 50, 66
Rosetta Stone 43
royal treasure 14, 16–17, 22–23
rubies 12

S

sacred treasure 7, 18–19
sacrifices 24
salvage 31
sapphires 12
Saqqara (Egypt) 46–47, 66, 67
Scythians 11, 15, 39, 66
ship burials 23
shipwrecks 6, 7, 15, 30–33, 48–49, 53, 60
shrines 7, 12, 18
Shwedagon pagoda (Yangon) 19
Sicán culture 6
silk 14, 17
silver 26, 33, 39, 49
sonar searches 48
space treasure 63
Spanish Armada 30
Spanish conquistadores 35, 40–41
Spanish treasure fleets 32
statues 27, 31, 39, 53, 55, 67

TUV

Templars 61
temples 18–19, 25, 29, 34
terra-cotta army 39, 55, 67
textiles 14, 15, 16, 17, 22, 23, 55
theft 56–57
Thirty Years' War 35
Tillya Tepe (Afghanistan) 23, 66
time capsules 50–51, 63
Titanic (liner) 31, 48, 68
tombs 6, 22–23, 38–39, 52
tools, archeological 44
torcs 26
Tower of London 56, 68
treasure seekers 42–43
treasure sites 66–67
treasure troves 52–53
treasuries 25, 28
Trojan War 60
Tutankhamun, Pharaoh 22
undiscovered treasure 60–61
Ur (Iraq) 14, 23, 50, 66, 67
Valley of the Kings (Egypt) 6, 14, 22, 39, 66
Varna (Bulgaria) 10, 66
Venice (Italy) 35
Vesuvius 29, 50
Vikings 7, 23, 27, 35, 66

WXYZ

waggoners 36–37
war damage 57
weapons, ornate 12, 16, 23, 25, 36
wishing wells 24
Xian (China) 39, 55, 66, 67
Zaraysk (Russia) 8, 66

Stone Age 8–9
Sun God 18–19, 24
Sutton Hoo (England) 55, 66

Acknowledgments

Dorling Kindersley would like to thank:
Sarah Owens for proofreading; Helen Peters for the index; David Ekholm JAlbum, Sunita Gahir, Jo Little, Sue Nicholson, Jessamy Wood, and Bulent Yusuf for the clip art; Sue Nicholson and Jo Little for the wall chart; and Camilla Hallinan and Dawn Henderson for editorial advice.

The publishers would like to thank the following for their kind permission to reproduce their photographs:

(Key: a-above; b-below/bottom; c-center; l-left; r-right; t-top)

akg-images: Brüning Museum, Lambayeque 66br; Landesmuseum Württemberg, Stuttgart/Erich Lessing 23cra; Erich Lessing 7cr, 51cr; Musée Guimet, Paris/Erich Lessing 18tl; Muzeul National de Istorie a României, Bucharest 26cl; National Museet, Copenhagen/Erich Lessing 51tr; **Alamy Images:** 19th Era 60bl; Bryan & Cherry Alexander Photography 62bl; Fabrice Bettex 17br; Sylvia Cordaiy Photo Library Ltd 21tl; Tony Cunningham 49br; Danita Delimont 23cr; Mary Evans Picture Library 36tr; Robert Harding Picture Library Ltd 41crb; Holmes Garden Photos 38bl; Angelo Hornak 28tl; Peter Horree 6bc; IML Image Group Ltd 34b; The London Art Archive 61bc; M. Timothy O'Keefe 24bl; Photos 12 19c; Rolf Richardson 35tr; Martyn Vickery 52cl; Ken Welsh 32bl; **Hizri Amirkhanov & Sergey Lev:** 8tl; **Courtesy of Apple.** Apple and the Apple logo are trademarks of Apple Computer Inc., registered in the US and other countries: 63cl; **The Art Archive:** 40bl; Bibliothèque des Arts Décoratifs, Paris/Gianni Dagli Orti 43ca; The British Library, London 43tr; Hermitage Museum ,St Petersburg/Gianni Dagli Orti 11tr; Historiska Muséet, Stockholm/Dagli Orti 9ca; Musée des Antiquités, St Germain en Laye/Dagli Orti 3tr, 8cl; National Anthropological Museum, Mexico/Gianni Dagli Orti 24bc, 24br; National Museum, Bucharest/

Gianni Dagli Orti 9tl, 34tr; **The Bridgeman Art Library:** Ancient Art and Architecture Collection/Private Collection 8-9bc; Boltin Picture Library 40-41c; Hermitage Museum, St Petersburg 15tr, 39cl; Museum of Fine Arts, Boston, Massachusetts/Gift of Mrs Frederick L. Ames 17r; Private Collection/Ken Welsh 39tl; Viking Ship Museum, Oslo/Giraudon 7l; Westminster Abbey, London 16r; **The Trustees of the British Museum:** 3c, 26-27tc, 46l, 55tc, 55tl, 58-59bc, 64-65 (Bkgd), 66-67 (Bkgd), 68-69 (Bkgd), 70-71 (Bkgd); **Corbis:** The Art Archive 10cl, 71bc; Asian Art & Archaeology, Inc. 9tr, 13c; Atlantide Phototravel 68b; Dave Bartruff 54tl; Bettmann 11br, 22cl, 35cl, 37tl, 41tl, 49tr; Jonathan Blair 7bc, 32-33bc, 44cl, 48-49bc, 51l; Blue Lantern Studios 36bl; Christie's Images 29tr; Elio Ciol 2cl, 13tr, 60-61c; Richard A. Cooke 66ca; EPA/Julian Aram Wainwright 25bl; EPA/Khaled El-Fiqi 47cla; EPA/Mike Nelson 47c, 47tr; EPA/Stephanie Pilick 4tl, 28bl; The Gallery Collection 20tr, 22tl, 38tr, 43tl; Godong/P. Deliss 45br; Goodlook Pictures/Philippe Giraud 35bc; Antoine Gyori 61tc; Robert Harding World Imagery/Gavin Hellier 69tl; Arne Hodalic 38b, 45cl; Hulton-Deutsch Collection 6cl; The Irish Image Collection 44tl; Hanan Isachar 18bc; Mimmo Jodice 66tl; Wolfgang Kaehler 19bl; Danny Lehman 67cb; Charles & Josette Lenars 67cb; Araldo de Luca 59tr; Micro Discovery 45c; Naturfoto Honal 27cr; Richard T. Nowitz 50tr, 69tr; Charles O'Rear 10tl; Gianni Dagli Orti 19tl, 24-25c; PAP/Krzysztof Éwiderski 69cb; Jose Fusta Raga 19bc; Reuters/Dept. of Museums & Antiquities, Malaysia 15br; Royal Ontario Museum 4cl; Solus-Veer 56cl; Gian Berto Vanni 1, 34tl; Visuals Unlimited 63br; Werner Forman 64tr, 67cl; Ralph White 31cr; Adam Woolfitt 49tl; Xinhua Press/Mike Nelson 47br; **Dorling Kindersley:** Courtesy of the Booth Museum of Natural History, Brighton 67cb; The British Museum, London 2cr, 3tl, 4cr, 4bl (Vase), 4br, 6tl, 10bc, 19tr, 24tr, 24cla, 26bc, 36c,

42b, 46tr, 58bl, 58c, 67tc; Sean Hunter 29br; © British Library Board. All Rights Reserved. (Picture Number 1022251.611) 4tr, 20bl; Judith Miller/Ancient Art 71tr; Judith Miller/Mendes Antique Lace and Textile 14c; Judith Miller/Sara Covelli 14bl; Judith Miller/Sylvie Spectrum 12bl (Pearls); Courtesy of the Musée de Saint-Malo, France 2c 36cl; Courtesy of The Museum of London 17bc, 36crb; Courtesy of the National Maritime Museum, London 23br, 36tl, 37b; Courtesy of the Natural History Museum, London/Colin Keates 12bl (Heliodor), 12bl (Ruby), 44c; Courtesy of the North Wind Undersea Institute, New York/Dave King 31bc; Wisdom Omoda Omodamwe - Modelmaker/Geoff Dann 43bc; Royal Pavilion Museum and Art Galleries, Brighton/Geoff Dann 16bl; St Mungo, Glasgow Museums/Ellen Howdon 71cl; Courtesy of the Statens Historika Museum, Stockholm/Peter Anderson 2bl, 27tr; By kind permission of the Trustees of the Wallace Collection, London 4bl(Spear), 35c, 53l; Michel Zabe 14-15bc; **ESA/CNES/ARIANESPACE:** 51br; **Mel Fisher Maritime Museum:** Dylan T. Kibler 32cr, 33br, 33c, 33crb, 33tl, 33tr; **Getty Images:** AFP 46-47bc, 67b; AFP/Aamir Qureshi 58tl; AFP/Don Emmert 15ca; AFP/Khin Maung Win 18cl; AFP/Louisa Gouliamaki 53tr, 54b; AFP/Michael Latz 55cr; Altrendo Travel 55br; The Bridgeman Art Library 2tr, 11l, 14tl, 17c, 23tl, 25r, 30cla, 39tr, 40cl, 50cl, 64bc, 65ca; Manuel Cohen 25tl; Cate Gillon 21tr; Hulton Archive 11cr, 20-21bc, 56cl; The Image Bank/Carolyn Brown 28-29c; Matt Moyer 39br; National Geographic/O. Louis Mazzatenta 45t; Newsmakers/William Thomas Cain 67t; Panoramic Images 18br; Scott Peterson 57cra; Photodisc/C Squared Studios 12c; Photodisc/Don Farrall 62tl; Reuters/Jason R. Zalasky 57tr; Stone/Jerry Alexander 29cr; Mario Tama 55tr; Time Life Pictures/Henry Groskinsky 13bl; Time Life Pictures/Mansell 42tl, 43br; Time Life Pictures/US Army 61br; **Wally Gobetz:** 63cr; © **Franck Goddio/Hilti Foundation:** 30-31cl;

C.F.W. Higham: 9br; **Foto Keltenmuseum Hochdorf/ENZ:** 23tr; **The Kobal Collection:** Werner Herzog Filmproduktion 41tr; **NASA:** JPL-Caltech/University of Arizona 63t; **Photolibrary:** Imagestate/The British Library, London 49cr, 70bl; Oxford Scientific/Konrad Wothe 13br; **Reuters/Eddie Keogh** 27bc; **Press Association Images:** AP Photo/Dario Pignatelli 52b; **Rex Features:** 57tr; Disney/Everett 48cl; Jonathan Hordle 52tl; Nils Jorgensen 59tl; Ian McCarney 56-57bc; SIPA Press 13bl, 56bl; Phil Yeomans 68cl; **Science Photo Library:** Hank Morgan 57tl; **TopFoto.co.uk:** Geoff Caddic 59crb; RIA Novosti 61tr; **Ulster Museum** ©2009: Photograph reproduced courtesy the Trustees of National Museums Northern Ireland 30bc; **Werner Forman Archive:** Courtesy Entwistle Gallery, London 15tl; Institute of Oriental Art, Chicago 65bc.

Wallchart: Alamy Images: Bryan & Cherry Alexander Photography (Seed Vault); **The Bridgeman Art Library:** Ancient Art and Architecture Collection Ltd (Bison Carving); Viking Ship Museum, Oslo/Giraudon (Viking Hoard); **Corbis:** Bettmann (Winged Collar); Jonathan Blair (Shipwreck); Hulton-Deutsch Collection (Howard Carter); Charles O'Rear (Crucible); Reuters/Department of Museums & Antiquities, Malaysia (Ming Pottery); **Dorling Kindersley:** The British Museum, London/Mike Row (Shark Tooth Necklace); Courtesy of the National Maritime Musem, London/James Stevenson and Tina Chambers (The Wallace Collection (Pike); **Getty Images:** AFP/Don Emmert (Violin); Altrendo Travel (Terracotta Warriors); The Bridgeman Art Library (Rhyton); Hulton Archive (Book of Kells); National Geographic/O. Louis Mazzatenta (Etruscan Pot); Time Life Pictures/Henry Groskinsky (Fabergé Egg).

All other images © Dorling Kindersley
For further information see: www.dkimages.com